Contents

THE LESSONS

Introduction

Number three—can you believe it?

If you've been along for the ride since volume one, you've become a cherished friend. I think of you often as I pound ideas into the computer, search for Scriptures that will speak clearly to kids, make piles of paper-sculpture "corpses" in search of just the right project, and try to envision what might go right (or wrong!) as you bring these lessons alive in your classroom.

Without your dedication to God's kids and your loving touch in the classroom, this book is nothing but a pile of paper and ink. Thank you so much for being a partner in ministry. It's an honor to serve you.

Once upon a time, there was a Christian education director who dreaded summer vacation. It's not that she objected to fun in the sun and that sort of thing; the problem was that when vacation arrived, Sunday school became exceedingly unpredictable. One week there would be eight kids in a class, and the next week there would be two. The following week somebody would bring 10 cousins, and kids would be hanging off the rafters. And, of course, the 10-cousins Sunday would be the day all the other teachers were out of town. What to do?

One day a very bright person in the congregation said, "Let's put all the kids together and do some kind of creative Bible lesson with the whole group." And then a series of wonderful things began to happen. Kids began to look forward to Sunday school because they knew it wouldn't be the same old out-of-the-book stuff. Little kids liked getting lots of attention from big kids. And big kids liked helping out and being looked up to.

The teachers really got into it too. Everyone signed up to teach one or two Sundays. The rest of the summer they could join an adult class or take some much needed R & R.

In fact, the concept of combined classes went over so well that the adults got a little jealous. So the Christian education director set up a couple of intergenerational lessons each summer and let the adults join in.

"Why save these combined classes for summer?" the teachers asked. Why indeed? So she began using combined classes whenever holidays, absences, or in-between Sundays presented a strategic dilemma.

The joyful, memorable learning experiences in those combined classes gave birth to *Sunday School Specials 1* and *2*—and now to *Sunday School Specials 3*. In this new book you'll find a whole quarter's worth of creative, combined-class Bible lessons you can use in the summer or any time at all! Each lesson contains an opening game or activity that grabs kids' attention and gets them tuned in to the theme; an interactive Bible story; a life-application activity and reproducible handout that help kids apply what the Bible says to their owns lives; and a challenging, meaningful closing.

This book includes sections on Old Testament stories, New Testament stories, and cele-

Sunday School Specials 3

by Lois Keffer

Group
Loveland, Colorado

Dedication

To Bob, Christy, Josh, and Sam,
who encourage me
and let me hog the computer.

Sunday School Specials 3

Copyright © 1995 Lois Keffer

Credits

Book Acquisitions Editor: Mike Nappa
Editor: Candace McMahan
Creative Products Director: Joani Schultz
Copy Editors: Patti Leach and Debbie Gowensmith
Art Director: Jean Bruns
Cover Art Director: Liz Howe
Designer: Dori Walker
Computer Graphic Artist: Kari K. Monson
Cover Illustrator: Diana Walters
Illustrator: Jeff Carnehl
Production Manager: Gingar Kunkel

Unless otherwise noted, Scriptures quoted from The Youth Bible, New Century Version, copyright © 1991 by Word Publishing, Dallas, Texas 75039. Used by permission.

Library of Congress Cataloging-in-Publication Data
(Revised for volume 3)

Keffer, Lois.
    Sunday school specials.

    1. Christian education—Textbooks for children.
2. Bible—Study and teaching. 3. Christian education of
children. I. Title.
BV15561.K38   1992   268'.432   91-36923
ISBN 1-55945-082-7 (v. 1)
ISBN 1-55945-177-7 (v. 2)
ISBN 1-55945-606-X (v. 3)

10 9 8 7 6 5 4 3 2 1   04 03 02 01 00 99 98 97 96 95

Printed in the United States of America.

brating special times. The four special times include a back-to-school lesson on peer pressure, as well as lessons for Thanksgiving, Christmas, and Easter. But you can use any of these lessons right now. Celebrate a joyous Christmas in July and focus one week on giving thanks. Any time is the right time to celebrate new life in Christ.

Within each lesson we'll let you know what to expect from kids of different ages and give you tips on how to get kids working together. Group's hands-on, active-learning techniques make it easy for you to capture and keep kids' interest. And you can be sure that the Bible lessons they learn will stick with them for a long time.

The Time Stuffer section shows you how to keep kids productively occupied before and after class and during their free moments. And you'll find special tips for gearing each Bible lesson to meet the needs of your particular group.

You have in your hands a wonderful tool that can help you solve your Sunday dilemmas. So go ahead and try something new. We want to help you make your Sunday school special!

Active Learning in Combined Classes

Research shows that people remember most of what they do, but only a small percentage of what they hear...which means that kids don't do their best learning sitting around a table talking! They need to be involved in lively activities that help bring home the truth of the lesson.

Active learning involves teaching through experiences. Students do things that help them understand important principles, messages, and ideas. Active learning is a discovery process that helps students internalize the truth as it unfolds. Kids don't sit and listen as a teacher tells them what to think and believe—they find out for themselves.

Each active-learning experience is followed by questions that encourage kids to share their feelings about what just happened. Further discussion questions help kids interpret their feelings and decide how this truth affects their lives. The final part of each lesson challenges kids to decide what they'll do with what they've learned—how they'll apply it to their lives during the coming week.

How do kids feel about active learning? They love it! Sunday school becomes exciting, slightly unpredictable, and more relevant and life-changing than ever before. So put the table aside, gather your props, and prepare for some unique and memorable learning experiences!

Active learning works beautifully in combined classes. When the group is playing a game or acting out a Bible story, kids of all ages can participate on an equal level. You don't need to worry about reading levels and writing skills. Everyone gets a chance to make important contributions to class activities and discussions.

These simple classroom tips will help you get your combined class off to a smooth start:
● When kids form groups, aim for an equal balance of older and younger kids in each

5

group. Encourage the older kids to act as coaches to help younger students get in the swing of each activity.

● In "pair-share," students work together with a partner. When it's time to report to the whole class, each person tells his or her partner's response. This simple technique teaches kids to listen and to cooperate with each other.

● If an activity calls for reading or writing, pair young nonreaders with older kids who can lend their skills. Older kids enjoy the esteem boost that comes with acting as a mentor, and younger kids appreciate getting special attention and broadening their skills.

● Don't worry about discussion going over the heads of younger students. They'll be stimulated by what they hear the older kids saying. You may be surprised to find some of the most insightful discussion coming literally "out of the mouths of babes"!

● Make it a point to give everyone a chance to shine—not just the academically and athletically gifted students. Affirm kids for their cooperative attitudes when you see them working well together and encouraging each other.

How to Get Started With *Sunday School Specials 3*

Lesson Choice

The lessons in *Sunday School Specials 3* are grouped in three units, but each lesson is designed to stand on its own. You're not locked into doing the lessons in any particular order. Choose the topics that best suit the needs of your class.

Several of the lessons contain suggestions for using an intergenerational approach—inviting parents and other adults in the congregation to join the class. You may want to schedule these lessons for special Sundays in your church calendar.

Teaching Staff

When you combine Sunday school classes, teachers get a break! Teachers who would normally be teaching in your 4- to 12-year-old age group may want to take turns. Or ask teachers to sign up for the Sundays they'll be available to teach.

Preparation

Each week you'll need to gather the easy-to-find props in the You'll Need section and photocopy one or more reproducible handouts. Add to that a careful read of the lesson and Scripture passages, and you're ready to go!

Time Stuffers

What do you do when kids arrive 15 minutes early? when one group finishes before others do? when there's extra time after class is over? Get kids involved in a Time Stuffer!

Each Time Stuffer needs just one preparation—then it's ready to use throughout the summer or whenever you're teaching these lessons. Choose the Time Stuffer that best appeals to the interests of your group or set up all three!

God's Garden

Make a God's Garden Wall and leave it up all summer. Make several photocopies of the "God's Garden" handout (p. 87). Let each student cut out a handout and write his or her name on the center flower. Have kids help you put up the flowers in a random design on a wall or in a hallway. Encourage kids to write friendship notes on each other's flowers and to add a flower each time the class has a visitor. Watch God's garden grow with loving comments and new "sprouts"! At the end of the summer, let kids take their flowers home.

Paper Wonders

Kids love paper folding and sculpture! Set out leftover photocopied handouts from lessons you've already taught. Kids will enjoy making extra crafts to give away to friends and to wow their families. You may want to make extra copies of all the handouts just for this purpose.

Vacation Board

You'll need a cork board, picture postcards, pushpins, and palm trees cut from construction paper. Mount the cork board at a height that's easily accessible to your youngest class members. Decorate it with construction paper palm trees and a few scenic postcards. Encourage kids to bring to class postcards, brochures, or drawings of places they have visited. Kids will have fun sharing their experiences and discovering what their classmates have been doing.

God Guides

LESSON AIM

To help kids understand that ★ God will guide us.

OBJECTIVES

Kids will
● search for a treat with the help of a guide who can't talk,
● hear how God guided Abraham,
● discover how to tune in to God's guidance, and
● make a commitment to follow God's guidance.

YOU'LL NEED

❏ a Bible
❏ chocolate kisses
❏ photocopies of Figures 1, 2, and 3 (pp. 17-19)
❏ gray, red, and tan construction paper
❏ scissors
❏ a 100-piece puzzle
❏ lunch bags
❏ razor knife
❏ photocopies of the "Life's Road Map" handout (p. 20)
❏ photocopies of the "God's Road Signs" handout (p. 21)
❏ paper
❏ markers

BIBLE BASIS

Genesis 12:1-7; 13:5-18

Abraham spent the first part of his life in the cities of Ur and Haran, centers of commerce, culture, and worship of the moon god.

Ruins of the famous ziggurat of Ur, a shrine to the moon god, can still be seen today. Somehow, in the midst of these cultural distractions, God got Abraham's attention and called him to leave his familiar surroundings and set out for an unknown destination in the wilderness of Canaan.

To his credit, Abraham wasted no time. At the age of 75, he gathered his family, possessions, herds, flocks, and servants and set out to follow the living God. All God told Abraham of his destination was that it was "the land I will show you" (Genesis 12:1). God attached a promise to his directions: He would make of Abraham's family a great nation through which all the people of the world would be blessed. Setting out in blind faith, Abraham followed God, his unseen guide. His willingness to hear and obey God resulted in the birth of two great nations and, ultimately, the Savior of the world, Jesus Christ.

Isaiah 55:9

At times even the most mature Christians struggle to understand what God is doing in their lives. Who hasn't looked toward heaven in frustration and asked, "Lord, how can this be part of your plan for me?" We would like God to submit a blueprint for our lives so that we could approve it or ask for revisions! God seldom shows us the whole picture but asks instead that we trust his supreme wisdom and love for us.

UNDERSTANDING YOUR KIDS

The cultural distractions Abraham faced pale in comparison to what kids face today. From the moment they wake in the morning until they click off their stereos at night, kids are bombarded with sophisticated messages from a culture that wants to convince them that material possessions and self-gratification bring happiness. In the midst of this media melee, how can kids learn to hear the quiet voice of God?

Typically our attention turns to God when we face a crisis. Natural disasters, financial problems, the serious illness of a loved one—all these things can call our attention away from the busyness of life and cause us to take a long look at our priorities and values. But it's even harder for children to think of how daily events impact their lives as a whole. Use this lesson to teach kids that life is a series of choices and that when they choose to stop and listen to God, God will always guide them toward the right choices.

The Lesson

ATTENTION GRABBER

Finders, Eaters

Help kids find partners, pairing older children with younger ones. Have each pair decide which person will leave the room and which person will stay. Say to the kids who are leaving: **You'll be the "finders." I'd like you to step out of the room for just a moment.**

Give each of the remaining partners two chocolate kisses. Say: **You'll be the "guides." These chocolate kisses are for you and your partner. Hide the two of them together somewhere in this room.** Give kids a few moments to hide their candy. When the candy is hidden, have the children line up facing you.

Say: **When your partners come back into the room, your job is to guide them to the candy you've hidden. But you may not use words, and you may not move your feet or your legs. Ready?**

Call in the finders and say to them: **While you were out of the room, your partner hid a treat for the two of you. Your partner's job is to guide you to that treat without using any words and without moving his or her feet. Your job is to pay close attention to your partner and see if you can figure out where he or she is trying to guide you. If you find the treat, bring it back to your partner and enjoy it together. Ready? Go!**

Allow a couple of minutes for partners to work together. Kids who don't know what to do may pick up on other pairs' tactics. Stop the game before anyone becomes too frustrated. Let guides retrieve any treats that haven't been found yet and share the treats with their partners.

When all the kids have their treats, clap your hands to bring everyone together. Ask:

● **Those of you who found your treats, what did your guides do to show you the way?** (Used hand signals; nodded his head; she pointed.)

● **Guides, what was it like not to be able to use words or move your feet?** (Frustrating; fun and challenging.)

● **What was it like if you weren't able to find your treats?** (I got a little worried; I couldn't figure out how other people found theirs.)

● **Who can tell about a time when you had a hard time finding your way somewhere?** (Once I had a hard time finding the way to my piano teacher's house; once I couldn't find my parents at the mall.)

● **Who can tell about a time you followed a guide—in**

TEACHER TIP

When you send kids out of the room, it's a good idea to give them something to do to occupy their time and keep them out of mischief. For instance, you might say, "Count backward from 100" or "Take turns telling about the nicest thing that happened to you this week."

10

a museum or on a hike or canoe trip, for instance? (We had a guide who took us on a nature hike at a state park; a guide showed us around an art museum.)

● **What's good about having a guide?** (Guides know a lot about places, so you learn a lot; with a guide you don't have to worry about getting lost.)

Say: **Today we're going to learn that ★ God will guide us. Our Bible story is about a man who took his whole family into the wilderness, following a guide he couldn't even see. Do you think you'd do that? Let's find out more about this brave man and his very special guide.**

BIBLE STUDY

Abraham's Journey (Genesis 12:1-7; 13:5-18)

Before class copy Figure 1, the ziggurat (p. 17), onto gray paper. Copy Figure 2, the altar (p. 18), onto red paper. Copy Figure 3, the town and the wilderness (p. 19), onto tan paper.

Open your Bible to Genesis 12 and explain that today's Bible story comes from Genesis, the first book of the Bible.

Fold the gray construction paper in half horizontally, along the dotted line.

Say: **Abraham lived in a big city called Ur. The people of Ur were very rich, and Ur was full of beautiful things. The most famous building in Ur was a ziggurat (ZIG-oo-rat). Can you say that with me? Ziggurat. Let me show you what the ziggurat looked like.**

Cut from A to B.

It was tall and wide and had lots of stairs going right up to the very top.

Open the center fold, then fold back on Line C so Figure 1 can stand by itself.

People went up the stairs to worship the moon god. That made God very sad. But Abraham wasn't like all the other people in Ur. Abraham worshiped the true God. He knew it was silly to worship the moon. Abraham knew that our God made the moon, the stars, and the whole beautiful world we live in.

One day God said to Abraham, "Leave this country and go to a new land that I will show you." Ask:

● **Do you think God gave Abraham a map? Why or why not?** (No, because God doesn't do things that way; no, Abraham could probably get a map somewhere else.)

● **Do you think God put up road signs in the wilderness? Why or why not?** (No, God probably decided just to tell Abraham where to go.)

● **Do you think Abraham felt a little scared about taking off into the wilderness without knowing where he would end up? Explain.** (He might have been a little scared, but he wouldn't have gone unless he trusted God.)

Say: **Abraham did exactly as God said. He packed up all his things on camels and said goodbye to the beautiful city of Ur.**

Set Figure 1 aside.

Abraham's family traveled hundreds and hundreds of miles to the new land where God wanted them to live. Ask:

● **How many of you have moved to a new place?**

● **Did you know where your new house was?** Let students respond.

● **What would it be like to move without knowing where you'd end up?** (Really scary; kind of weird.)

Say: **Week after week they traveled through the hot desert. Every day Abraham trusted God to show him where to go. Finally Abraham and his family arrived in the land of Canaan. God spoke to Abraham again and said, "I will give this land to you and to your children." Abraham was glad to be in the new land God had promised to show him.**

Fold the red construction paper vertically along the dotted line and cut from A to B.

Abraham was glad to be far away from the ziggurat where people worshiped the moon. In Abraham's new land, everyone would worship God.

Cut from B to D. Then open the center fold and fold back on Line C. Hold up Figure 2 with the fire folded back, out of sight.

Abraham took big stones and built an altar to God. Then Abraham built a fire on the altar and worshiped God.

Fold forward on Line C so the fire appears.

When Abraham traveled to the land of Canaan, he took everything he owned. Abraham was very rich! He had lots of tents, lots of silver, lots of gold, and herds and herds of animals.

Abraham's nephew Lot traveled with Abraham. Lot was rich, too. So with all of Abraham's sheep and Lot's sheep, there wasn't enough grass and water to go around, and their servants started to fight.

Pick up the tan construction paper.

The fighting made Abraham sad. He knew that God didn't lead him to a new land to start a fight. So he called Lot and said, "Our people shouldn't be fighting. Just look around."

Fold the tan construction paper in half on Line A.

"There's plenty of land here for everyone. So you choose where you want to go. Then I'll go the other way." Because Abraham was older, he could have said, "I'm the head of the family, so I'll pick first." But Abraham trusted God to

guide him, so he let Lot pick first.

Cut from B to C.

Lot looked to the east. Guess what he saw.

Unfold the paper, then fold back on Line D so just the city shows.

He saw a beautiful valley with a city.

Refold on the center line and turn the paper over.

Then Lot looked to the west.

Cut from E to F. Then unfold the paper and fold back on Line G so just the wilderness is showing.

Lot saw a wilderness with rugged hills, not too much water, and no cities. What do you think Lot chose?

Turn the paper so the city is showing.

Lot chose the beautiful valley with the city. But that didn't bother Abraham at all. Abraham knew God would guide him, so he was happy to live in the wilderness. God did guide Abraham, and he became the father of many nations. Thousands of years later, Jesus was born from Abraham's family.

★ **God will guide us just as he guided Abraham. And when we follow God, great things can happen in our lives.**

(Adapted from *Clip & Tell Bible Stories,* copyright © 1995 Lois Keffer. Published by Group Publishing, Inc., Box 481, Loveland, CO 80539.)

LIFE APPLICATION

Pieces of the Puzzle

Purchase a jigsaw puzzle of not more than 100 pieces. Or glue a medium-sized poster to a sheet of poster board, then cut it into puzzle pieces. This activity works best with a fairly complex picture rather than a large, simple image. Before class, separate the puzzle pieces into four piles. Put each pile of pieces in a lunch bag.

Say: **Abraham trusted God completely, even when it meant leaving his home and traveling hundreds of miles in the wilderness. Let's have some fun finding out why we can trust God just as Abraham did.**

Help kids form four groups. The groups don't have to be exactly the same size, but it's helpful to have a similar number of older and younger children in each group. Hand a bag of puzzle pieces to each group and designate separate areas of the room where groups can work.

Say: **In your bag you'll find a puzzle. I'll give you a couple of minutes to put your puzzle together. As soon as you're absolutely sure you know what's pictured on your puzzle, raise your hands. I'll come to your group so that you can whisper it to me.**

TEACHER TIP

If you have more than 20 students, use two puzzles and have four groups work on each puzzle.

13

Give groups a minute or two to work on their puzzles. Since each group has just a portion of the puzzle, it's unlikely that any group will be able to guess what the finished picture will be. Before students get frustrated, call everyone together and ask:

● **Why haven't you been able to figure out your puzzle?** (Some pieces must be missing.)

Say: **Then it looks like we'll have to get all the groups together to complete the puzzle. I'd like each group to choose one representative to bring your puzzle pieces and work on finishing the puzzle.**

Indicate a table or open floor space in the middle of the room where the four representatives can put the puzzle together. Invite the rest of the students to stand behind and offer help and encouragement. When the puzzle is finally completed, have a big round of applause. Then gather everyone in a circle and ask:

● **Why did everyone have to work together to figure out what picture was on this puzzle?** (Because we all had parts of it; because no group had enough pieces.)

Say: **That's kind of the way life is. We just see little pieces of the picture, a day at a time. We don't know what our lives will be like a year from now or even a day from now. But God does. Listen to what God says in Isaiah 55:9: "Just as the heavens are higher than the earth, so are my ways higher than your ways and my thoughts higher than your thoughts."** Ask:

● **What does that verse mean to you?** (That God knows more than we do; that God can see everything, and we can see only a little.)

Say: **God has given us good minds, but we can see and understand only a little. On the other hand, God sees and knows everything about us. And on top of that, God loves us very much. That's why we—like Abraham—can trust that ★ God will guide us. God sees the whole picture and wants to guide us in ways that are best for us. That means we need to trust God, even when we don't know exactly how things are going to turn out. Now let's look at some different ways to tune in to God's guidance.**

COMMITMENT

Life's Road Map

Make enough photocopies of the "Life's Road Map" handouts (p. 20) for each student to have one. Before class, use a razor knife or rotary cutter to open the dashed-lined slits marked on the handouts. You'll also need one photocopy of the "God's Road Signs" handout (p. 21) for every two students. Cut the road signs apart and sort them into four piles.

Write the numbers 1 through 4 on four separate sheets of paper and place them at four different locations in the room. Set all the copies of Road Sign 1 by the number 1, all the copies of Road Sign 2 by the number 2, and so on.

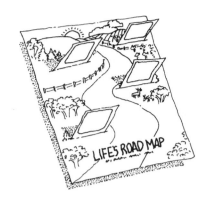

Give each student a copy of the "Life's Road Map" handout. Have students count off by fours. Send the ones to Road Sign 1, the twos to Road Sign 2, the threes to Road Sign 3, and the fours to Road Sign 4.

When students have gathered by the appropriate road signs, say: **Choose a reader and a discussion leader for your group. The reader will read your road sign aloud. Then you'll all fold your road signs and push them through the slits marked on your "Life's Road Map" handouts. When your road signs are in place, the discussion leader will ask: "How can we do what these verses teach us?" After a few minutes, I'll clap my hands, and everyone will rotate clockwise to the next road sign.**

Circulate among groups to answer questions and offer ideas and encouragement. After two or three minutes of discussion, clap your hands and have groups rotate. Repeat the process two more times so each group collects and discusses all four road signs. Then clap your hands to bring everyone together. Ask:

● **How can we be sure that ★ God will guide us?** (Because God guided Abraham; because the Bible tells us that God will guide us.)

● **What did you learn about how to tune in to God's guidance?** (We need to pray; we should study the Bible; Christian teachers can help us; we need to decide to follow God.)

Say: **Those are all good things, and they will all help you discover God's guidance. Right now, turn to a partner and tell him or her what you'll do this week to follow God.**

Allow a few moments for partners to share.

CLOSING

On Our Way

Say: **I hope you'll keep your road map and review what the Bible verses teach you to do. When we do our best to follow God, we can be sure that ★ God will guide us. When you go home, share your road map with your family and tell them what you learned about how God guides us.**

Here's a fun song that will help you remember the things we learned today. Lead children in singing this song to the tune of "Yankee Doodle."

God will guide us every day
And show us what to do.
Just as God led Abraham,
God will guide us, too.

Decide that you will follow God;
Read the Bible carefully.
Pray and listen every day
And learn from what your teachers say.

Close with a prayer similar to this one: **Dear God, thank you for guiding Abraham. Please guide us and help us follow you this week. In Jesus' name, amen.**

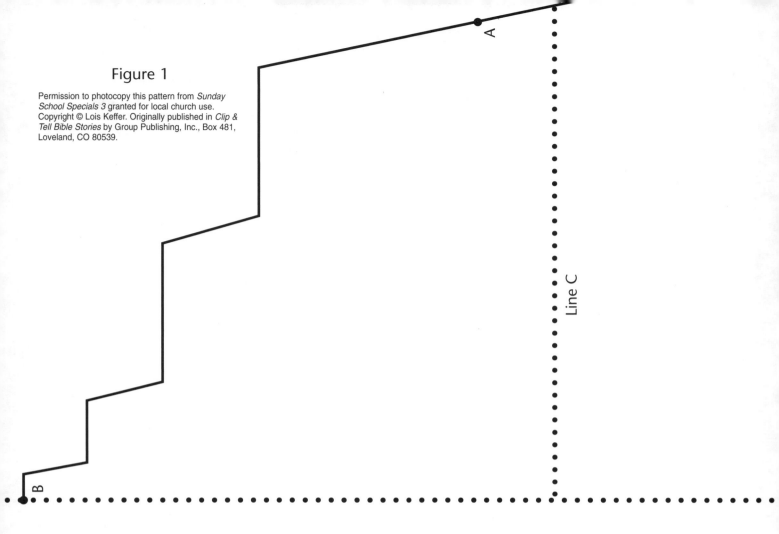

Figure 1

A

B

Line C

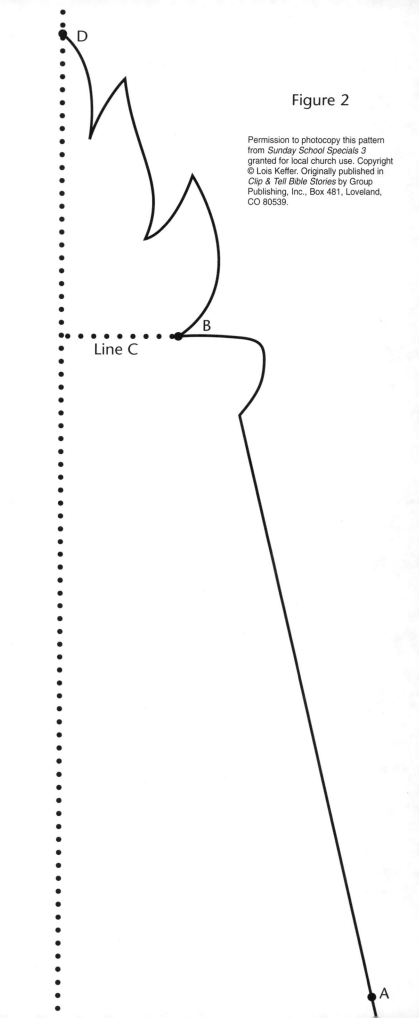

Figure 2

Line C

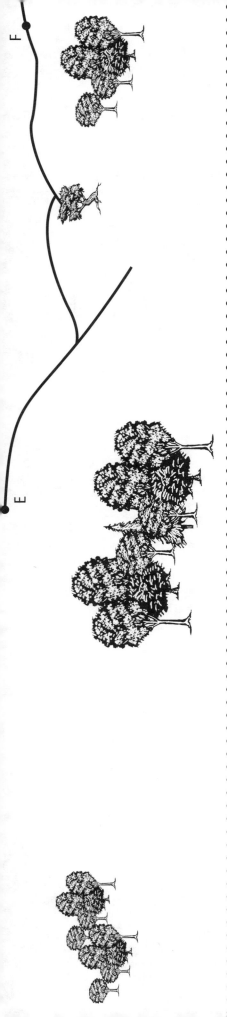

Figure 3

Line G

Line A

Line D

F

E

B

C

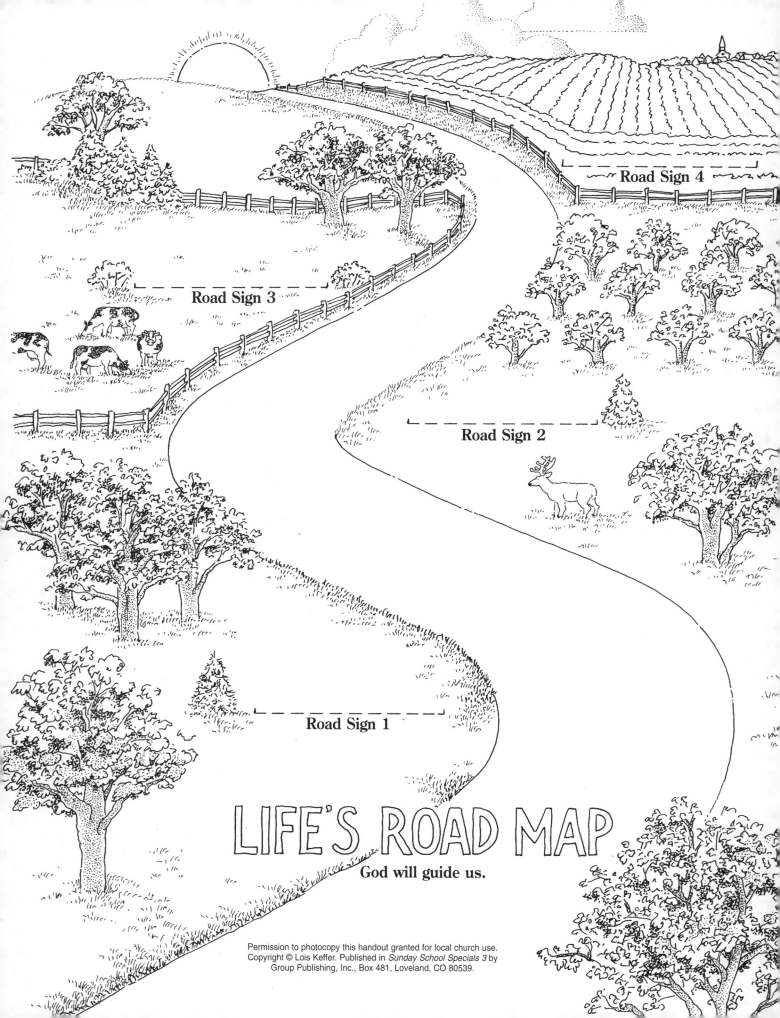

Road Sign 4

Road Sign 3

Road Sign 2

Road Sign 1

LIFE'S ROAD MAP

God will guide us.

GOD'S ROAD SIGNS

1. DECIDE TO FOLLOW GOD.

"Trust the Lord with all your heart, and don't depend on your own understanding. Remember the Lord in all you do, and he will give you success" (Proverbs 3:5-6).

2. READ GOD'S WORD.

"Your word is like a lamp for my feet and a light for my path" (Psalm 119:105).

3. PRAY AND LISTEN TO GOD EVERY DAY.

"If you go the wrong way—to the right or to the left—you will hear a voice behind you saying, 'This is the right way. You should go this way' " (Isaiah 30:21).

4. LEARN FROM CHRISTIAN TEACHERS.

"Listen carefully to what wise people say" (Proverbs 22:17a).

"Jesus said to all of them, 'If people want to follow me, they must give up the things they want. They must be willing to give up their lives daily to follow me' " (Luke 9:23).

"All Scripture is given by God and is useful for teaching, . . . for teaching how to live right" (2 Timothy 3:16).

"But when the Spirit of truth comes, he will lead you into all truth" (John 16:13a).

"Let the teaching of Christ live in you richly. Use all wisdom to teach and instruct each other by singing psalms, hymns, and spiritual songs with thankfulness in your hearts to God" (Colossians 3:16).

1. DECIDE TO FOLLOW GOD.

"Trust the Lord with all your heart, and don't depend on your own understanding. Remember the Lord in all you do, and he will give you success" (Proverbs 3:5-6).

2. READ GOD'S WORD.

"Your word is like a lamp for my feet and a light for my path" (Psalm 119:105).

3. PRAY AND LISTEN TO GOD EVERY DAY.

"If you go the wrong way—to the right or to the left—you will hear a voice behind you saying, 'This is the right way. You should go this way' " (Isaiah 30:21).

4. LEARN FROM CHRISTIAN TEACHERS.

"Listen carefully to what wise people say" (Proverbs 22:17a).

"Jesus said to all of them, 'If people want to follow me, they must give up the things they want. They must be willing to give up their lives daily to follow me' " (Luke 9:23).

"All Scripture is given by God and is useful for teaching, . . . for teaching how to live right" (2 Timothy 3:16).

"But when the Spirit of truth comes, he will lead you into all truth" (John 16:13a).

"Let the teaching of Christ live in you richly. Use all wisdom to teach and instruct each other by singing psalms, hymns, and spiritual songs with thankfulness in your hearts to God" (Colossians 3:16).

2 Can You Believe It?

LESSON AIM

To help kids understand that ★ sometimes God surprises us.

OBJECTIVES

Kids will
● succeed at a seemingly impossible feat,
● hear Sarah tell how God surprised her,
● be challenged to trust God to do the impossible, and
● commit to looking for God's surprises.

YOU'LL NEED

❑ a paper sack of small prizes
❑ a bowl of raw potatoes
❑ plastic drinking straws
❑ Bibles
❑ a photocopy of the "God's Good Surprises" handout (p. 33)
❑ photocopies of the "Surprise Pop-Up" handout (p. 34)
❑ markers
❑ glitter glue
❑ scissors
❑ tape

Genesis 18:1-15; 21:1-3

Among fascinating Bible heroines, Sarah certainly holds her own. Think about her life. She willingly followed Abraham from the culturally advanced city of Ur to an unknown destination in a wilderness hundreds of miles away. She went along with Abraham's cowardly schemes to pass her off as his sister so he wouldn't be killed for his beautiful wife. When she proved to be barren, she urged Abraham to have a child by her servant girl. Sarah certainly can't be faulted for lack of courage!

Having been barren during her childbearing years, Sarah must have given up all hope of having Abraham's son. When she was old enough to be a great-great-grandmother, three strangers appeared near Abraham's tents. The Bible text suggests that at least two of the visitors were angels, and the third is referred to as "the Lord" (18:10). When the Lord stated that Sarah would have a child before the year was out, Sarah laughed audibly. But she didn't have the last laugh, for despite Sarah's doubts, Isaac made his appearance as predicted.

Luke 18:27

The concept of "impossible" doesn't lie within God's modus operandi. You'll find it all in the Bible—from speaking the world into existence, parting the sea, and making the sun stand still to raising people from the dead. God can do the impossible today just as he did centuries ago.

UNDERSTANDING YOUR KIDS

It's a sad fact of life that kids need to be skeptics by the time they're ready to start school. "Don't talk to strangers." "Don't believe everything you hear on TV." "Walk away from anyone who tries to give you money or candy." "Don't listen to most of what's on the radio." Kids and parents know that a certain amount of skepticism is healthy and necessary.

Here's the good news: We don't have to urge kids to be skeptics when it comes to believing in God. The Bible is true—always. God keeps his promises—always. God can do anything—period. Ain't it great? Use this lesson to teach children to expect the unexpected from our incredible God.

The Lesson

ATTENTION GRABBER

Do the Impossible

You'll need a small prize for each child, such as a pack of sugarless gum or a coupon for an ice-cream cone. Hide the prizes in a paper sack and set the sack out of sight.

Set out a bowl of raw potatoes and a stack of plastic drinking straws. You'll need one potato and one straw for each child. You may want to scrub the potatoes so kids don't soil their clothes.

As kids arrive, give them each a potato and a straw.

Say: **I have a great prize for anyone who can poke a straw clear through a potato. No fair using a knife or breaking your potato. I'll give you a minute or two to see if you can accomplish this amazing feat. Remember, there's a prize to be won, so give it your best shot!**

Give kids a couple of minutes to try to get their straws through their potatoes. If anyone succeeds, tell him or her not to let anyone else know how to do it. If no one succeeds, have children set their straws and potatoes aside.

Say: **I guess I'll just have to keep the prizes for myself. Or I could let you in on the secret of how to do this trick.** Let the kids egg you on. Then say: **Oh, all right. I guess since I'm such an amazingly wonderful teacher, I'll show you how to do it. But before I do, I need to know something.** Ask:

● **Do you believe I can poke a straw through this potato? Why or why not?** (No, because if we couldn't do it, you can't either; no, because a straw isn't strong enough to go through a potato; yes, because you've read about how to do it.)

Say: **Stand up if you think I can poke this straw through this potato. OK, now I'll need a drumroll from everyone who's standing. Pat your hands on your legs while your truly amazing teacher performs this truly amazing feat.**

Cover the top of the straw with your thumb and poke it through the potato in one firm stroke.

Then say: **Wow! That really is amazing, isn't it? I guess since I'm the only one who did it, I should keep the prizes for myself. No? OK, here's how you do it: Cover the top of the straw with your thumb and hold it there tightly as you punch the straw through.**

Help each child accomplish the trick, then pass out the prizes. Have children set their potatoes, straws, and prizes by one wall of the room. Explain that they can take these things home after class and show the trick to their families. Ask:

● **Do you think this is an amazing trick? Explain.** (Yes,

TEACHER TIP

It's actually quite easy to poke a straw through a potato. Simply cover one end of the straw with your thumb. The pressure created by the trapped air keeps the walls of the straw rigid. Practice this trick before class so you can perform it confidently in front of the kids.

because a straw doesn't seem strong enough to go through a potato; no, because the air inside the straw helped it go through.)

● **When you came to class today, did you think you'd end up poking a straw through a potato?** (No, I didn't know what we'd do; no, I thought we'd hear a Bible story.)

● **Were you surprised when you were able to push your straw through your potato? Why or why not?** (Yes, because it sounds impossible; no, because I saw you do it.)

● **Do you think I'm a truly amazing teacher? Why or why not?** (Yes, because you do cool tricks; no, because anyone who read about the trick in a book could do it.)

Say: **Well, the truth is, I'm not so amazing. The directions for doing this are in our lesson for today. Anyone could read the book and learn to do the trick. But I know someone who *is* truly amazing.** Ask:

● **Who do you think that might be?** (God; Jesus.)

Say: **Our story today is about our truly amazing God and how he did something that surprised everyone. In fact, what God did was much more surprising than poking a straw through a potato. We're going to hear the story from a very old woman named Sarah. Sarah found out that ★ sometimes God surprises us. I want you to treat Sarah like a respected guest when she comes to our class.**

BIBLE STUDY

Sarah's Surprise (Genesis 18:1-15; 21:1-3)

Say: **Sarah lived a life full of adventure. She and her husband, Abraham, left their life in the city and traveled hundreds of miles to the land of Canaan, where God wanted them to live. God promised Abraham that he would be the father of many nations and that there would be as many members of his family as there are stars in the sky.**

But there was just one problem. Years and years went by, and Sarah never had a baby. Finally Abraham and Sarah were old enough to be great-great-grandparents, but they still didn't have a child. Sarah must have given up hope. But she found out that ★ sometimes God surprises us. Let's hear the rest of the story from Sarah herself. Look! Here she comes now!

Have "Sarah" say: **Thank you for inviting me to your class today. I want to tell you about the biggest surprise of my life. You can help me tell my story by watching me carefully and doing the same actions I do.**

After the poem, have Sarah wave goodbye as the kids give her a round of applause. Then ask:

TEACHER TIP

You may want to invite an older woman or someone from your congregation who's a good actor to visit your class in Bible costume to read the poem "Sarah's Surprise" (pp. 31-32). Or simply drape a shawl around your head and shoulders and read the poem yourself. Hint: Kids really enjoy hearing a male teacher read in a quavery, grandmotherly voice.

● **What was Sarah's surprise?** (God let her have a baby; she got to have a baby even though she was old.)

● **Why did Sarah laugh when she heard one of the visitors say she would have a baby in a year?** (Because she was too old to have a baby; because she had given up on having a baby.)

Say: **The Bible tells us that the three visitors Sarah talked about were not ordinary people. They may have been angels. The Bible even calls one of them the Lord. Ask:**

● **Why do you suppose God waited so long to give Abraham and Sarah a baby?** (So they would know it was a special baby; so only God could make it happen.)

Say: ★ **Sometimes God surprises us. God doesn't run on clocks and calendars as we do. God has all the time in the universe. Abraham and Sarah worried about getting older and not having a baby, but they were thinking about "people time," not God's time.**

Let's take a few minutes to think about how God might surprise people today.

LIFE APPLICATION

Angels in Africa

Say: **A few years ago, God surprised some people in the country of Kenya. Listen carefully and see if you can tell how God surprised the people in this story.**

Missionary children from all over Africa attend the boarding school at Kijabe mission station in the beautiful country of Kenya. Kijabe is one of the largest mission stations in the world.

One night several years ago, the missionaries at Kijabe noticed a huge fire at a neighboring village not more than two miles away. Orange and yellow flames licked at the night sky, signaling danger. A friend from the burning village ran to the mission station with the terrifying news that the rebel Mau Mau tribe had attacked and burned the village, and they were coming to Kijabe next!

The missionaries gathered to pray. They had only a barbed wire fence and one policeman to protect themselves and the missionary children from the attacking Mau Maus.

Pause at this point and ask:

● **How do you think God will surprise the people in this story?** Let several children guess, then continue with the story.

TEACHER TIP

You may want to choose a mature, confident reader to read this story. Sometimes hearing a different voice helps kids who are growing restless refocus on the lesson.

The missionaries prayed all night. As dawn broke quietly over the Kenyan countryside, the residents of Kijabe could hardly believe they hadn't been attacked.

No one knew why the Mau Maus didn't attack that night. The story finally came out when some of the rebels were captured.

"We planned to attack Kijabe," the Mau Maus confessed, "but when we got close, guardians blocked our way."

The police were still bewildered. There were no soldiers at Kijabe that night. And besides, the Mau Maus wouldn't have been afraid to fight soldiers.

"The guardians we saw were giant, flaming figures," the Mau Maus explained. "We were terrified, and we all ran away!"

Ask:

● **Who did God surprise in this story?** (The missionaries and the Mau Maus.)

● **How did God surprise the Mau Maus?** (By sending flaming guardians to block the road and protect the mission station at Kijabe.)

● **How did God surprise the missionaries?** (God kept them from being attacked when they knew attackers were on their way.)

● **What do you think the giant, flaming figures were?** (Angels; helpers from God.)

● **If you had been at Kijabe that night, what would you have learned?** (That God is powerful; that we don't know what God will do; that God can surprise us.)

Distribute Bibles and say: **Let's see what the Bible says about what God can do.** Have children look up Luke 18:27. Encourage readers to share their Bibles with nonreaders. Ask a volunteer to read the verse aloud. Then ask:

● **What does this verse teach us about God?** (That God can do anything; that nothing is too hard for God.)

Say: **Isn't it great to know that God can do anything? And because he can do anything, ★ sometimes God surprises us! When we're in a tough situation, we may not be able to think of a way out—but God can! Sarah couldn't think of a way she could have a baby when she was so old, but God did it! The missionaries at Kijabe couldn't think how one policeman and a barbed wire fence could protect them from attacking Mau Maus, but God knew what to do.**

We always need to remember that God is bigger, wiser, and more powerful than we are, so God can surprise us. Let's see if we can think of ways God might surprise kids today.

Form three groups and give each group one of the situation cards from the "God's Good Surprises" handout (p. 33). Make sure you have a good balance of readers and nonreaders in each group.

Say: **Each group needs a reader who will read your situation aloud, a discussion organizer who will encourage everyone to share ideas, and a reporter who will tell the whole class about your ideas. Brainstorm at least three ways God might surprise the people in your situation. You've got three minutes. Go!**

Circulate among groups as they work, encouraging discussion and offering ideas. Here are some possible outcomes for each situation.

Situation One: Alyssa might find a really great friend who lives on the same street her grandma does. If the grandma lives on a farm, Alyssa might be able to have the horse she's always dreamed of. Alyssa might find a club at her new church where she makes lots of new friends.

Situation Two: Matt might find out that two of the kids are really nice after all; they've just been following the lead of another boy. The assistant principal might realize that he's put Matt in a difficult situation and decide to move Matt right away. Matt might discover that the boys aren't mean after all, and they could end up being friends.

Situation Three: A truck driver might stop and help the dad fix the car right on the spot. A policeman might radio for a tow truck so the car could get fixed quickly and the family could be on their way. The car might have broken down right in front of a farmhouse owned by people who are friendly and helpful.

After two minutes, clap your hands and announce that kids have one more minute for discussion. After one more minute, clap your hands and bring everyone together. Ask the reader from the first group to read that group's situation, then have the reporter tell the group's ideas of how God might surprise the person in that situation. Invite the rest of the class to add their ideas. Repeat this process for the second and third groups.

Say: **Congratulations! Those are great ideas. You're really catching on to the fact that even when things seem impossible, ★ sometimes God surprises us.**

COMMITMENT

Surprise Pop-Up

Say: **Let's make reminders to help us be on the lookout for God's surprises every day.**

Distribute photocopies of the "Surprise Pop-Up" handout (p. 34).

Be sure you've made a sample pop-up card before class so kids can see how the three-dimensional card works.

Set out markers, glitter glue, scissors, and tape. Encourage kids to decorate the handout creatively then cut the paper in half horizontally on the solid line. The top half of the handout becomes the card base; have kids set it aside for a moment.

Have kids fold the bottom of the handout in half, then cut from point A to point B and unfold the present. Have them cut a slit on the solid line from the bottom of the page to the dotted line then fold forward on the dotted line. Show kids how to tape the bottom sections that are folded forward to the shaded area of the card base. When the card base is folded, the present disappears. When the card base is opened, the present pops up. As kids are working on their pop-up cards, encourage them to tell about times God has surprised them. Have kids who finish early help clean up the paper scraps and put the art supplies away.

When everyone is finished, have kids form pairs.

Say: **Tell your partner where you'll put this pop-up card so it can remind you to watch for God's good surprises.**

Give kids a moment to share. Then ask:

● **Why does God surprise us?** (Because God loves us; because God knows so much more than we do.)

● **Does God always make difficult situations turn out the way we want them to? Explain.** (No, because God is wiser than we are; no, not for me.)

Say: **God isn't like a genie or a fairy godmother, so God doesn't always make things turn out the way we wish they would. Then again, sometimes God makes things turn out better than we ever thought they could. The important thing to remember is that God is all-powerful—he can do anything. And God is all-wise—he knows what's best for us. And God's love for us is bigger than the universe, so we can always trust him to make things turn out for the best.**

CLOSING

God's Surprises

Ask:

● **What was the impossible problem Sarah faced in our Bible story today?** (She couldn't have a baby.)

Say: **We also talked about some big problems kids today might face, such as a parent losing a job, moving away from friends, scary things at school, and having a car break down. I wonder if anyone here today is facing a problem that seems impossible that you'd like to have us pray about.**

TEACHER TIP

If you've never used glitter glue before, give it a try! You'll find it wherever rubber stamps are sold. The glue and glitter are combined in a squeeze bottle with a narrow tip so you have all the fun of glitter with none of the mess. For quick drying, set the paper in the sun or use a blow-dryer.

TEACHER TIP

If you sense that a child is troubled about a problem, you can approach the child in a nonthreatening manner after class. Gently ask, "Is there anything you'd like to talk with me about?" Respect the child's right to refuse. Just by asking, you've shown that you're concerned, and you've laid the groundwork for the child to approach you in the future.

If your kids are open and comfortable with each other, invite them to share their concerns with the class. If kids aren't used to being together, they may prefer to talk to you individually after class.

Say: **It's great to know that we don't have to come up with solutions to problems that seem impossible. Our God is great and powerful and loving, and ★ sometimes God surprises us. Let's thank God for that right now.**

Pray: **Lord, thank you for the great God you are. Thank you for being wise and powerful and for loving us. Help us to look to you and trust you to surprise us. In Jesus' name, amen.**

Remind children to take their potatoes, straws, prizes, and pop-up surprise cards home. Encourage them to use these items to tell their families about today's lesson.

Sarah's Surprise

(based on Genesis 18:1-15; 21:1-3)

I was sitting inside my tent one day
When three strangers passed our
way.
(Walk three fingers across palm.)

My husband, Abraham, bowed
low,
For these were important men, you
know.
(Bow.)

He said, "Please rest and wash your
feet
While my wife and I fix something
to eat."

So they sat down beneath a tree,
And Abraham came to talk to me.

(Cup hands around mouth and whisper loudly.)
"Please make some bread. Be
quick! Let's hurry!"
So I jumped up and worked in a
flurry.

"Flour, salt, and a little yeast,
Now help me stir—we'll make a
feast."
(Pretend to stir.)

Abraham cooked a tender roast.
Don't you think he's quite a fine
host?
(Put hands on hips and nod proudly.)

The guests enjoyed the food we
made
While Abraham stood close by in
the shade.

"Where's your wife, Sarah?" one
man asked.
When I heard my name, I stopped
and gasped.
(Gasp.)

Abraham answered, "In the tent
over there."
Then I began to listen with care.
(Cup hand to ear.)

"I'll come back next year," said
guest number one.
"And when I come back, she'll
have a son."
(Fold arms and nod.)

"A son?" I thought. "But I'm too
old!
I'll never have a baby to hold."
(Shake head.)

"My husband and I are wrinkled
and gray.
No child for us! No baby! No way!"

"A son? Oh, no! Ha-ha! Hee-hee!"
I felt the laughter rising in me.
(Hold stomach and laugh.)

"A son? At my age? It must be a joke!"
I laughed so hard I started to choke.

Laughter made tears roll down my cheek
(run finger down cheek),
But then our guest began to speak.

"Why does she laugh about having a son?
By this time next year, it will be done!"
(Shake finger.)

"I didn't laugh, sir." I was scared, so I lied.
"Oh yes, you did," our guest replied.
(Nod head.)

Finally our guests went on their way,
But I tell you, I'll never forget that day.
(Shake head.)

Can you tell what happened? I'll give you a clue.
What our visitor said really came true!

Before the year was past and done,
I gave birth to a beautiful son!
(Pretend to hold baby.)

You've never seen such a fine little boy.
He was Abraham's pride and joy.
(Fold arms and nod.)

We named him Isaac—that means "laughter."
Because we lived happily ever after.
(Cross hands over heart.)

Now listen to me because I am wise.
You've learned how God gave me a huge surprise.

And someday God may surprise you, too
(point at a child),
For there isn't anything God can't do.

GOD'S GOOD Surprises

Photocopy and cut apart the situations. You will need one situation for each group of three students.

Alyssa was sure this was the worst day of her life. Her dad had lost his job a year ago. He'd found some temporary work, but it didn't pay very well. Finally Alyssa's parents decided to sell their house and move 300 miles away to live with Alyssa's grandma. Alyssa would have to go to a new school where she didn't know anyone.

How might God surprise Alyssa?

There had been a lot of trouble in the lunchroom at school lately, so the assistant principal decided to assign seats. "The seat you get today is where you'll stay for the rest of the year," he announced. Matt couldn't believe it when he was assigned to a table with some of the meanest kids in the whole school. "This is horrible," Matt thought. "I have to sit with these guys for the rest of the year!"

How might God surprise Matt?

Alex and Stephanie's parents had been promising all summer that the family would go on a canoe trip. Now they were finally on their way. But just an hour from home, their car broke down. "We'll never get our canoe trip," Alex moaned. "Why did this have to happen now?"

How might God surprise Alex and his family?

Tape present here.

What is impossible with men is

POSSIBLE

with God

(from Luke 18:27).

B

SURPRISE!

Line C

A

God Makes a Hero

LESSON AIM

To help kids understand that ★ God is more powerful than anything or anybody.

OBJECTIVES

Kids will
- be challenged to do difficult tasks,
- participate in a lopsided tug of war,
- celebrate Gideon's victory, and
- make a commitment to rely on God's power.

YOU'LL NEED

- ❏ three lunch bags
- ❏ two large safety pins
- ❏ three balloons
- ❏ two bananas
- ❏ a plastic knife
- ❏ several self-adhesive bandages
- ❏ transparent tape
- ❏ star stickers
- ❏ several feet of rope
- ❏ scissors
- ❏ straight pins
- ❏ ribbon
- ❏ photocopies of the "Power Pinwheel" handout (p. 45)
- ❏ plastic drinking straws
- ❏ a hole punch
- ❏ a large electric fan

BIBLE BASIS

Judges 6:1–7:23

Gideon's story begins with a sad tale of oppression. The Israelites lived in fear of their stronger Midianite neighbors, who had a nasty habit of swooping down at harvest time to plunder and ruin the Israelites' crops. Judges 6:5 says the Midianite invaders covered the land like "swarms of locusts." God's people were left in such poverty by these systematic attacks that they cried to the Lord for help. God chose Gideon for the job.

Gideon is a hero after my own heart. An angel found him threshing wheat under cover of a wine press, hoping to save his meager harvest from invaders. The angel hailed Gideon, saying, "The Lord is with you, mighty warrior!" Excuse me—a warrior in a wine press? Just so! God was about to put in motion a most unlikely series of events that would free Israel from the Midianite threat, make Gideon a national hero, and restore the hearts of a wayward people. Sometimes, perhaps just to remind us where the real power lies, God chooses to use a meek man rather than a muscleman!

2 Corinthians 12:9b-10

"When I'm weak, then I am truly strong." This is the sort of paradox that makes non-Christians scratch their heads and stare. But what a glorious fact for those who do believe! When we're drained, demoralized, and in over our heads, we finally throw ourselves on God's mercy. That's precisely when miraculous things begin to happen.

UNDERSTANDING YOUR KIDS

Overwhelmed. That's the perfect word to describe today's kids. Have you, at any time in the last year, spoken to a child who had time to be bored? Did you ever think you'd see the day when a fifth-grader was panic-stricken at having misplaced her planning calendar? Have you seen the teeny-weeniest little ones bravely sawing their Suzuki violins at the mall? Both parents and kids are guilty of cramming life so full that there's barely time to stop and take a deep breath. Why? Nobody wants to miss out. Little League, after all, lasts only a few years. And if kids don't start gymnastics (music lessons, soccer, ballet, football) early, they'll never be competitive. Kids who aren't on the go as much as their neighbors tend to feel second-rate. And we adults certainly don't want our kids to miss any of the memorable experiences of childhood! For most kids today, the pressure never lets up. They might welcome the idea of hiding in a wine press!

Your students will love meeting Gideon. They'll laugh at his deplorably low self-esteem. They'll gasp when God whittles down his army. And they'll cheer when the 90-pound weakling with God's power in his afterburners chases the bad guys all the way across the river. This story is good news for kids who are so maxed out that it's an act of heroism just to get up in the morning.

ATTENTION GRABBER — The Lesson

Triple Challenge

Before class, gather three lunch bags. In bag one, place three uninflated balloons and a large safety pin. In bag two, place two unpeeled bananas and a plastic knife. Place several adhesive bandages in bag three. Place a roll of transparent tape and another large safety pin in a conspicuous place in the room.

Put star stickers on kids as they arrive. Put a sticker on the cheek of the first person, on the hand of the second person, and on the nose of the third person. Continue in this manner so that one-third of the group has cheek stickers, one-third has hand stickers, and one-third has nose stickers. As you're placing stickers, keep a balance of younger and older students in each group.

After everyone has arrived, say: **Welcome to our Triple Challenge! I can see that you're all stars, so you shouldn't have any trouble meeting my challenges! To get started, I'd like you to form three groups—the cheeks, the hands, and the noses. All the people with hand stickers meet over there, people with cheek stickers meet over there, and people with nose stickers meet over there.**

When groups have gathered, take bag one to the cheeks and say: **Your challenge is to poke a pin into an inflated balloon without popping the balloon.** Take bag two to the hands and say: **Your challenge is to slice an unpeeled banana without slicing the skin of the banana.** Take bag three to the noses and say: **Your challenge is to stick out your tongue and touch your nose. As you're practicing, please be careful not to injure yourselves.**

Now you all have your supplies. If you see anything else in the room that might help you, feel free to use it. I'll give you three minutes to accomplish your challenge. I'm sorry, but I won't be able to answer any questions during the three minutes. Go!

If students approach you with questions, steadfastly refuse to answer. After three minutes (or earlier if one group seems inclined to give up), call time by clapping your hands, then ask each group to report. If any group accomplished its challenge, give the group a round of applause. To groups that couldn't accomplish their challenges, say: **You know, the challenges I gave you are easier than they seem.**

Demonstrate how to meet each challenge. Before sticking a pin into an inflated balloon, place a piece of transparent tape over the place where you'll insert the pin. To slice an unpeeled banana without slicing its skin, poke a pin into the banana at one-inch intervals and wiggle the pin back and forth. When you peel the banana—voilà! It's already sliced. To stick out your tongue and touch your nose, stick out your tongue, then touch your nose with a finger.

Say: **See? That wasn't so hard!** Ask:

● **How did you feel when I gave you your challenge?** (Hopeless; like I could never do that.)

● **What went through your mind when I showed you how simple it is to accomplish each challenge?** (I couldn't believe it; I was amazed.)

Say: **Our Bible story today is about a man who felt a lot like you did when I first presented the challenges. Let's find out what his challenge was and how this man found out that ★ God is more powerful than anything or anybody.**

BIBLE STUDY

Lopsided War (Judges 6:1–7:23)

Hold up a rope and say: **I'd like to begin our Bible story with a game of Tug of War. Who would like to play?** Choose several of the smallest volunteers to form one team and several bigger kids to form the other team. Have the teams take positions on either end of the rope. Ask:

● **Does anyone have an idea of how this match might turn out?** (The bigger kids will win; the little kids might win if they ate spinach for breakfast.)

Say to the players: **Ready, set—oops! I almost forgot something.** Point to the first member of the smaller team and say: **I think you can handle this job by yourself. I'd like the rest of the people on your team to drop the rope and sit down.** Now there should be one small child facing several bigger children.

Say: **Good! That's better. I like the way this game is shaping up.** Ask:

● **Given the way the contest is set up right now, what**

are the chances that (name of smaller child) **will win?** (Almost none; not unless a miracle happens.)

Say: **This is how it was when the hero of our Bible story went to war. The odds didn't look good at all. Let's see what happened. First I'll need someone to be Gideon.** Choose a volunteer. **Now I'll need someone else to be an angel.** Choose a second volunteer. **You bigger kids will be the Midianites. Choose a captain for your team. You smaller kids will be the Israelites. Gideon will be the captain of your team.**

Have the teams stand facing each other. Have Gideon and the angel stand beside you. Put the rope away so that it won't distract the children as they act out the Bible story.

Say: **As I read the Bible story, the captains will show or tell you how to act it out. Gideon, in addition to being the captain of your team, you'll act out what Gideon does. Angel, listen carefully for your part and be ready to act out what you hear. OK, troops, we're about to go into battle, so pay careful attention to what your captains say and do.**

Read "The 'Who, Me?' Hero" (pp. 40-41). Use lots of drama and perhaps a bit of melodrama in your reading. Keep an eye on the captains and offer suggestions if they need help directing their teams to act out the story.

Finish the Bible story with a hearty round of applause. Then ask:

● **How was this Bible story like the tug of war we set up earlier?** (One side was much stronger; the odds seemed hopeless.)

● **Why do you think the Lord kept telling Gideon to send men home?** (Because he wanted to see if Gideon trusted him; God wanted to use his own power to defeat the Midianites.)

● **Why did God choose an ordinary man like Gideon to lead his people?** (Because an ordinary man would have to trust God; because God didn't need a powerful leader.)

● **What would you have thought of Gideon's plan if you had been one of the 300 soldiers who stayed to fight?** (I'd have thought he was nuts; I'd probably have wished I'd been sent home too.)

● **Do you think God is just as powerful today as he was in Gideon's day? Why or why not?** (Yes, because God never changes; no, because you don't hear stories like that today.)

Say: **God took an ordinary, frightened young man and turned him into a hero. God used an army of 300 men to defeat an enemy with more than 100,000 soldiers. The night of that battle, God's people learned that ★ God is more powerful than anything or anybody. And God never changes. God can help us today just as he helped Gideon long ago.**

The "Who, Me?" Hero

(based on Judges 6:1–7:23)

It was a dark time in the nation of Israel. The Israelites never knew when powerful Midianite soldiers would ride in on camels to kill people, steal their livestock, and ruin or steal their crops. There were so many enemy soldiers that it was hopeless for the Israelites to even try to fight back. Seven years of constant raids left the Israelites poor and starving. Finally they cried out to God for help.

God had a plan. The plan involved a young Israelite named Gideon. Gideon was an ordinary young man who was just as afraid of the Midianites as anyone else. In fact, he was threshing his wheat in a wine press, hoping that Midianite soldiers wouldn't find him there.

Suddenly an angel appeared to Gideon and said, "The Lord is with you, mighty warrior!"

Gideon asked, "If the Lord is with us, why are we having so much trouble with the Midianites?"

The Lord said, "Go with the strength you have and save Israel. I am sending you."

"But, Lord," Gideon answered, "how can I save Israel? I belong to the smallest family of one of the weakest tribes, and I'm the least important member of my family!"

The Lord said, "I will be with you, and you will strike down the Midianites!"

Gideon replied, "If you're really pleased with me, give me proof. Please wait here until I bring you an offering."

The angel agreed to wait, so Gideon hurried to prepare a meal, then placed it on a rock near where the angel was sitting. The angel touched the food with the tip of his staff, and fire jumped out of the rock and completely burned up the food! Then the angel disappeared.

"I've seen the angel of the Lord face to face!" Gideon exclaimed. Then he built an altar and worshiped God.

Some time later, the Midianites and their allies massed their troops to form a huge army of well over 100,000 men. They camped in a valley, waiting for just the right moment to attack Israel. When Gideon heard of this threat, God's Spirit came upon him. Gideon blew his trumpet and called for the fighting men of Israel to join him. Gideon led Israel's army to a valley south of the Midianite army. Both camps prepared for battle.

Then the Lord said to Gideon, "You have too many men! I don't want your soldiers to brag that they defeated the Midianites in their own strength. Tell any soldier who is afraid that he can go home." Gideon did as the Lord said, and 22,000 men went home, leaving Gideon only 10,000 soldiers.

Then the Lord said to Gideon, "There are still too many men. Take them down to the water for a drink. Send home any man who gets down on his knees to drink."

Gideon did just as the Lord commanded. Almost all the men got down on their knees to drink. Gideon sent them home. That left him with only *300 soldiers!*

God said, "With these 300 men I'll save you and help you defeat the Midianites." Gideon trusted God and prepared to go into battle with only 300 men.

In the middle of the night, God told Gideon to take his servant and sneak into the enemy camp, where most of the soldiers were resting in their tents. Gideon climbed down to the valley, then tiptoed to the edge of the Midianite camp. It was *huge!* There were more soldiers and camels than anyone could count. What could his little army of 300 men do against more than 100,000 soldiers?

Gideon and his servant crept so close to an enemy tent that they could hear the soldiers talking. One soldier was telling another that he'd dreamed that a loaf of bread rolled into the camp and knocked the tent over flat. The other soldier said, "Your dream is about the sword of Gideon. God will use him to defeat our whole army!"

Gideon and his servant scurried back to their own camp. "Get up!" Gideon ordered. "The Lord has handed the army of Midian over to you!"

Gideon made sure each of his soldiers had a trumpet and a clay jar with a burning torch inside it. Under cover of darkness, Gideon's 300 men quietly surrounded the enemy camp. On Gideon's signal, each man blew his trumpet and shouted, "For the Lord and for Gideon!" Then they smashed their clay jars and let the torches burn brightly.

The sneak attack threw the enemy camp into a panic. The enemy soldiers began fighting each other. Then Gideon and his men chased them far from the land, and God's people lived in peace for many years.

LIFE APPLICATION

Scary Stuff

Have kids arrange chairs in a semicircle and sit facing you. Ask:

● **What was Gideon doing when our story began?** (Hiding in a wine press; trying to keep his wheat from getting stolen.)

Say: **Gideon was hiding, and he was scared to death. Let's learn a rap that reminds us of how God changed Gideon from a scaredy-cat to a hero. Here's how the first part of the rap goes. I'll say a line, then you repeat it after me.**

Standin' in a wine press *(cross fists over heart)*,
Shaking with fear *(shake all over)*,
Hoping there's no enemy *(cup hands around eyes and look
  around)*
Sneakin' round here. *(Tiptoe in place.)*

Repeat the rap once or twice until kids are comfortable with the words and actions.

Then say: **I don't know about you, but there have been plenty of times in my life when I felt scared, outnumbered, and ready to run in the other direction, just like Gideon. All of us get scared by different things. I'm going to read a list of scary things. If what I read wouldn't scare you at all, just remain seated. If it would scare you a little bit, stand up. If it would scare you a whole lot, stand up and wave your arms over your head. When I read something really scary, I should feel a breeze from all the arms waving. Let's do our rap once more as a reminder of how scared Gideon was at the beginning of the story.**

Standin' in a wine press *(cross fists over heart)*,
Shaking with fear *(shake all over)*,
Hoping there's no enemy *(cup hands around eyes and look
  around)*
Sneakin' round here. *(Tiptoe in place.)*

Read the following list, pausing after each item for kids to respond. Say: **Show how you would feel...**

● **just before a math test.**

● **when you have to walk home past the meanest kids in the neighborhood.**

● **when you have to play an instrument or sing in front of lots of people.**

● **when your family's car breaks down on a long trip.**

● **during a spelling bee.**

● **when a gang of kids makes fun of you on the play-ground.**

● **when you have to give an oral report.**

● **when you're home alone at night.**

● **when a parent is having trouble at work.**

● **when you wake up with a bad dream.**

● **when you are called to the principal's office.**

● **when there's a really bad storm and the lights go out.**
Ask:

● **Does anyone want to tell about another time you felt really scared?** Allow children to share.

Say: **That's all pretty scary stuff. We know that Gideon was scared at the beginning of the story.** Ask:

● **What changed Gideon from a scaredy-cat to a hero?**

(God did; God sent an angel to him; God let him hear how scared the enemy soldiers were.)

Say: **There's a verse in the New Testament that helps us understand what happened to Gideon. Listen to 2 Corinthians 12:10: "I am happy when I have weaknesses, insults, hard times, sufferings, and all kinds of troubles for Christ. Because when I am weak, then I am truly strong."** Ask:

● **What kinds of insults and hard times did Gideon face?** (Enemies stole his crops; he was afraid of being invaded; he had to hide his food from enemy soldiers.)

● **How did Gideon discover that when he was weak, then he was truly strong?** (When he couldn't do anything, God took over; he learned to trust God's power.)

● **What does "when I am weak, then I am truly strong" mean to you?** (That I can do anything with God's power; that I'm strong when I let God take over.)

Say: **Let's learn the second part of the Gideon rap. This part tells about Gideon, the hero.** Teach kids this rap line by line, then repeat it once or twice until they're comfortable with it.

Look at all our enemies *(point)*
Shakin' with fear. *(Shake all over.)*
When this battle's over, they'll know *(make fists)*
God was here! *(Shake finger and point to the sky.)*

Say: **We can look to God for strength just as Gideon did. God's not looking for musclemen and heroes. God's looking for ordinary people who believe that ★ God is more powerful than anything or anybody.**

COMMITMENT

Power Pinwheels

Set out scissors, transparent tape, straight pins, 18-inch lengths of ribbon, photocopies of the "Power Pinwheel" handout (p. 45), plastic drinking straws, and a hole punch. Before kids begin to work, point out Ephesians 6:10 at the top of the handout and read it aloud. Then ask students to read it aloud with you. (Young nonreaders will have heard you read the verse, so they'll be able to "read" along with the older kids.)

Say: **Think of all the different ways you can be strong in the Lord. When you've thought of a way, stand up and make a muscle, like this.** Flex your biceps.

Kids might mention ways such as reading the Bible, praying, tuning in to God's plan, asking others to pray with them, counting on God's strength instead of their own, and trusting God

TEACHER TIP

Make your own Power Pinwheel before class so you'll be familiar with the process. To make really dazzling pinwheels, purchase holographic wrapping paper. Let students use the handout as a pattern to cut their pinwheels from the sparkling paper.

even when they're scared. Ask:

- **What gives power to turn a pinwheel?** (The wind.)
- **Where does the wind come from?** (The weather; from God.)

Say: **These pinwheels will remind us to count on God's power, not on our own.**

Have kids work in "power pairs" to make their pinwheels. Have each child find a partner who was on the opposite team during the Bible story. As children finish, challenge them to blow on their pinwheels to see how quickly and steadily they can make their pinwheels turn.

Then set a large electric fan on a table and turn it on high. Let the kids hold up their pinwheels to catch the wind from the fan. After a few moments, stop the fan and ask:

- **How was the wind from the fan like God's power?** (It's stronger than our own power; it does more than we could ever do.)

Say: ★ **God is more powerful than anything or anybody. Turn to your partner and tell one way you'll rely on God's power this week.**

Allow a minute or two for partners to share. Then call everyone together and ask kids to tell what their partners said they would do to rely on God's power.

CLOSING

Blown Away

After everyone has shared, gather kids in a circle and have them raise their Power Pinwheels high. Close with a prayer similar to this one: **Dear Lord, sometimes your power blows us away! You helped Gideon change from a scaredy-cat to a hero. You defeated a huge army with only 300 men. Help us to remember that ★ you're more powerful than anything or anybody and that we can rely on your power when we face scary things. In Jesus' name, amen.**

"Be strong in the Lord and in his great power" (Ephesians 6:10).

1 Cut out the square, then cut in on the diagonal lines. (Be sure not to cut all the way to the center.)

2 Fold two opposing corners marked with arrows to the center and secure them with a tiny piece of transparent tape.

3 Do the same with the other two corners.

4 Push a straight pin through the center of the pinwheel and into one end of a plastic drinking straw.

5 Experiment and adjust the pin so the pinwheel moves freely but doesn't flop around.

6 Pinch the other end of the straw and make a hole in it with a hole punch. Thread and tie several lengths of ribbon through the hole.

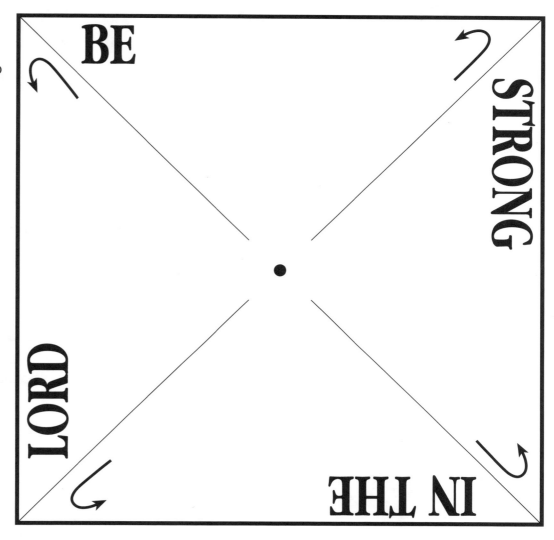

4 The Turn-around Prophet

LESSON AIM

To help kids understand that ★ God wants us to obey him.

OBJECTIVES

Kids or families will
● experience frustration when a teammate doesn't follow instructions,
● learn about Jonah's struggle to obey,
● identify times it's difficult for them to obey, and
● commit to obeying God.

YOU'LL NEED

❑ a marker
❑ two blindfolds
❑ a large box fan
❑ a spray bottle filled with water
❑ a dirty rag
❑ Bibles
❑ paper
❑ pencils
❑ chalkboard and chalk or newsprint
❑ scissors
❑ glue sticks or transparent tape

NOTE

This lesson works well with an intergenerational class. You may wish to invite whole families to join you for this session.

❑ photocopies of the "Tumbling Pyramids" handout (p. 56)
❑ a bag of treats

BIBLE BASIS

Jonah 1:1–4:11

As you prepare for this lesson, put this book away for a moment, open your Bible, and treat yourself to a quick read of the four short chapters that constitute the book of Jonah. Adventure on the high seas—what a plot! Jonah went to great lengths to avoid God's assignment, but God went to greater lengths to reel in the reluctant prophet. Jonah's objections to preaching in Nineveh were not without basis. For the Jews, encouraging the people of Nineveh to find and follow God could almost be considered a breach of national security. Nineveh's military strength posed a constant threat to God's people. Even though Israel's borders were fairly strong and secure in Jonah's time, most Jews viewed God's potential destruction of an enemy city as a positive thing. The Jews (and Jonah himself) seemed to glory in their "favored nation" status with God and cared little for what happened to people outside their borders.

When God told Jonah to go preach repentance to his enemies, Jonah chose to cut and run. Three days in solitary confinement (you can't really count the fish as a companion) helped Jonah adjust his attitude. When the fish spewed the indigestible little prophet out onto the sand, Jonah followed through on God's command. But Jonah was anything but overjoyed when the people of Nineveh reacted with sackcloth, fasting, and prayers of repentance. As Jonah pouted outside the city, God shook him by the shoulders a second time. "Don't you get it, Jonah? I love these people!" The account ends as God makes this point, but we don't know Jonah's final reaction. We can at least give Jonah credit for obedient actions if not altogether obedient attitudes. (Before I shake my finger at Jonah, I think I'll go see what I can do about this log in my own eye.)

John 15:10-11

Jesus knew the cost of obedience. Yet, just before his death, Jesus promised his followers that obedience would result in God's loving presence and the "fullest possible joy."

UNDERSTANDING YOUR KIDS

I wanna do what I wanna do when I wanna do it. Children seem to evidence that attitude within a day or two of exiting the

47

womb, if not before. In children's defense, they do spend most of their early years living out other people's agendas. The frustration of very young children may spill over into tears and tantrums; as kids grow older, we see a range of behaviors from grudging cooperation to full-fledged rebellion.

Children can't wait to grow up—to be the boss. Most children have the mistaken impression that adults always get to do exactly what they want to do. Ha! Use this lesson with an intergenerational class to help children see that adults—and famous Bible characters—sometimes struggle with obeying God's commands. They'll also discover that God doesn't give up on us but keeps drawing us back into the circle of his love.

The Lesson

ATTENTION GRABBER

The Tail of the Whale

As students arrive, form teams by using a marker to put a fish mark on the first person's hand and a heart on the second person's hand. Continue alternating fish and hearts until everyone's hand is marked. It's not necessary for teams to be equally matched. Have the "fish" and the "hearts" form separate groups.

Say: **I need one volunteer from each team to step out of the room and be blindfolded.**

If you have adults in your class, choose adult volunteers. Give each of the volunteers a blindfold. As they step out of the room and blindfold each other, give these instructions to both teams: **Your job is to form yourselves into the shape of a whale. You can do it any way you want—just figure out how to make yourselves into a whale. But leave a space where the whale's tail should be. When your blindfolded team member comes back into the room, you'll tell him or her how to join you and finish up the tail of your whale. When your teammate has joined you and your whale is complete, shout, "This whale has a tail!" The members of the team that finishes first will get a one-minute back rub from the members of the other team.**

As the teams form themselves into whale shapes, step out of the room and make sure the volunteers' blindfolds are tied securely. Tell the heart volunteer to follow his or her team's directions quickly. Tell the fish volunteer to wander around the room and ignore his or her teammates' directions.

Bring the volunteers back into the room and tell the teams to begin shouting their directions. Be sure to guard the safety of

the blindfolded students. After the heart volunteer has helped the hearts complete their whale, call time and have the fish give the hearts one-minute back rubs.

Then say: **Time's up!** Gather everyone around you and ask:

● **How did you like this game?** (I didn't like it because our volunteer didn't follow our directions; I liked it because we got back rubs.)

Ask the fish volunteer:

● **Why did you ignore what your teammates said?** (Because you told me to; because that's what I was supposed to do.)

Say: **Right. I told you to ignore your teammates' instructions because I wanted us all to see what can happen when one person doesn't obey.** Ask the fish team:

● **What happened when your teammate didn't obey you?** (We lost the game; we had to give back rubs to the other team.)

Say: **Because your teammate didn't obey you, you lost the game and lost a chance to win a back rub. Just to make things fair, I'll have the hearts give the fish a one-minute back rub right now.** Pause as members of the heart team pair up with members of the fish team and begin giving back rubs.

Say: **No one wants to miss out on something good like a back rub. When one person fails to obey, lots of people may end up paying the consequences. That is one reason ★ God wants us to obey him. Our Bible story today is about a man who was determined not to obey God, just as** (name of fish volunteer) **was determined not to obey** (his or her) **teammates. But what was at stake was much more than a back rub. A whole city and the lives of all its people were at stake. Let's get right to our Bible story and see what happens.**

BIBLE STUDY

The Turnaround Prophet (Jonah 1:1–4:11)

Say: **I'd like half of the hearts to form a boat shape on the left side of the room. The fish can make a big fish shape again here in the middle.** Make sure the fish and the boat are a few feet apart. **The other half of the hearts can stand over there by the wall on the right side of the room. You'll be the people of Nineveh. Our volunteer who wouldn't follow directions will be Jonah. Jonah, you stand next to the boat.**

Good! Now we're almost ready to begin our Bible story. But first, let me ask you this:

● **What country would you consider to be our worst enemy today?** (Iraq; China.)

● **How would you feel about going and telling the people of** (name of country) **how much God loves them and wants to forgive them?** (I'd be scared to go there; I might go, but I wouldn't like it too much.)

Say: **Well, God asked Jonah to go and preach in an enemy city. The Jews were afraid of the powerful people in Nineveh, and Jonah didn't want to go there. I'm going to read a poem that tells Jonah's story. As I read, listen carefully and act out your part. Here we go!**

Set a large box fan on the floor so it will blow on the "boat." Have a spray bottle full of water ready. Read "The Turnaround Prophet" (pp. 51-52). As you read, be ready to prompt people to act out the events in the story.

After you've finished reading the story, have students give themselves a big round of applause. Then gather everyone around you and ask:

● **Why didn't Jonah want to obey God?** (Because he didn't like the people of Nineveh; he didn't want to go there because they were his enemies.)

● **What might have happened to the people of Nineveh if Jonah hadn't gone there to preach?** (God might have destroyed them; something terrible might have happened to their city.)

● **Why did God want Jonah to preach in Nineveh?** (Because God loved those people and didn't want to destroy them; because God loves everyone and wants everyone to love him back.)

Say: ★ **God want us to obey him. Because Jonah obeyed, the whole city of Nineveh believed in God!**

LIFE APPLICATION

I Hate It When . . .

Ask:

● **Have you ever felt like Jonah—when you knew what was right and what you should do but you really didn't want to do it?** Allow students to respond.

● **Why do we get ornery and stubborn?** (Because we're not perfect; because there are other things we'd rather do; sometimes we don't feel like doing what we're told.)

● **What was the last thing you had to do that you really didn't want to do?** (Clean my room; help with the dishes; mow the lawn.)

Have everyone stand in a circle. Hold up a dirty rag and say: **This dirty rag stands for things that we really don't want to do. When the rag is tossed to you, finish this sentence: "I**

The Turnaround Prophet

(based on Jonah 1:1–4:11)

God talked to Jonah
And let him know one day
To head on out to Nineveh
And go right away!

Though Jonah wasn't friendly
With the people over there,
God wanted him to tell them
To watch and beware!

*(Cue the people of Nineveh to look
   mean and nasty.)*
Evil filled their nights,
And bad things filled their days.
God wanted him to warn them now
To change their ways!

Jonah heard quite clearly
The things God had to say,
But the stubborn prophet thought,
"I don't want to obey!

"Those people aren't my friends.
I won't preach there—no way!
Instead of doing what God said,
I think I'll run away."
*(Cue Jonah to run and hop into the
   boat.)*

So Jonah packed a bag,
And then he grabbed his coat;
He hurried down to Joppa,
Where he hopped aboard a boat.

Once he got on board the ship,
Jonah went below.
He thought, "No one can find me
   here;
Not even God will know.

"I think I'll take a little nap;
This spot seems safe and warm."
But little did old Jonah know
That God would send a storm.

The sky turned dark and scary,
And the wind began to blow;

The waves seemed big as mountains
As the boat heaved to and fro.
*(Turn the fan on high. Squirt water
   into the breeze made by the fan.)*

The captain said to Jonah,
"Wake up! Wake up, stranger.
Please start praying to your God.
Our ship is in great danger!"

The sailors asked, "Oh, Jonah,
Is this storm your fault?"
"Yes," he said, "here's what to do
To make the storm halt.

"You see, I ran away from God;
I came on board to hide.
But since God sees me, you must
Throw me over the side!"

"We must toss poor Jonah in!
Heave-ho!" cried the crew.
Then they prayed, "Forgive us, Lord,
We want to please you."
*(Cue the boat people to gently push
   Jonah out. Turn off the fan.)*

When Jonah hit the water,
He sank down...down...down.
And in the darkness of the sea,
He thought he'd surely drown.

But God was watching Jonah;
To save him was God's wish.
So from the dark depths of the sea
God sent a giant fish.

The fish swam up to Jonah
And with one mighty "Gluup!"
It opened up its giant jaws
And swallowed Jonah up!
*(Cue the fish people to "swallow"
   Jonah.)*

"My goodness!" Jonah cried out.
"I'm in a fish—I think.
It's very wet and dark in here

51

And surely does stink!

"But can it be God's rescued me?
It seems that I'll survive.
Even though I've disobeyed him,
God's kept me alive!"

Jonah knew just what to do;
He knelt right down to pray.
"Forgive me, God, for I have sinned"
Was all that he could say.

Jonah stayed three days and nights
As the fish's guest.
He prayed, "Lord, when you let me out,
I'll do what you think best."

God told the fish to turn around
And swim toward the land.
Then with one giant hiccup,
Jonah landed on the sand!
*(Cue the fish people to gently push
    Jonah away.)*

He shook himself and looked around
And said, "I'm back! Hooray!
Now I must go to Nineveh,
For I promised I'd obey."

So when he reached that city,
God told him what to say.
"You must leave your sinful ways
And turn to God today."
*(Cue Jonah to walk to Nineveh and
    preach to the people.)*

"God will ruin your city—
He's already set the date.
So pray and tell God you're sorry
Before it's too late!"

The people listened to Jonah.
They knew what he said was true.
They cried and prayed all day long
And even skipped dinner, too!
*(Cue the people of Nineveh to kneel
    and pray.)*

The Ninevites believed in God.
They knew they had been wrong.
They started obeying what God
    said—
It didn't take them long.

So God forgave the people
For the bad things they had done.
Then the whole town was happy—
All, that is, but one.

It was Jonah who was angry.
He could not understand
Why God would forgive the people
Of such an evil land.

Sitting by a shady vine,
Jonah began to pout.
"Why would God forgive those folks?
I just can't figure it out."
(Cue Jonah to sit and pout.)

The very next day, God sent a worm
To eat away Jonah's vine.
Then Jonah cried, "Why did you take
    that away?
It was shady! It was mine!"

God spoke again to Jonah
And said, "Listen to what I say.
You care a lot for your shady vine
Though I made it in only a day.

"Well, I care for the people of
    Nineveh,
Just as I care for you.
If I forgave you for your sins,
I can forgive them, too."

There's a lesson to be learned here,
So remember as long as you live
That God always loves us, in spite of
    our sins,
And that when we ask, he'll forgive.

hate it when..." For instance, you might say, "I hate it when I have to go to bed early" or "I hate it when I have to pay my income tax." Everybody ready?

Begin by finishing the sentence yourself, then toss the rag to someone else. Encourage students to toss the rag to those who haven't had it yet.

After everyone has had a turn, set the rag out of sight. Ask:

● **Do you think anyone in the whole world gets to do what he or she wants to do most of the time? Explain.** (No, most people have to work or go to school, and they don't have much time for anything else; yes, maybe some rich people get to do what they want to do.)

● **Do you think doing what you want to do all the time would make you happy? Why or why not?** (Yes, that would be awesome; no, I'd probably get bored.)

Say: **Let's find out what Jesus said about obeying God. We'll also find out what really makes people happy.**

Form groups of four. Give each group a Bible, paper, and a pencil. Have groups choose two readers, a reporter, and an encourager. Write these Scripture references on a chalkboard or newsprint: "John 14:15-16" and "John 15:10-11". Instruct the readers to read the passages aloud to their groups. Then read these questions one at a time, allowing discussion time between each question:

● **Who can name a time Jesus obeyed God even though it was hard?** (When Jesus died on the cross; when Jesus took our sins.)

● **How does God help us obey him?** (He sends us a "Helper"; he gives us his love.)

● **According to Jesus, what brings joy?** (Being in God's love; obeying God and feeling his love.)

● **Jesus promises us wonderful joy if we obey his commands. What are some of Jesus' commands to us?** (To love and obey God; to love each other; to forgive people.)

Call the groups together and invite the reporters to share what they learned from the Scripture passages and from their discussions.

Then say: **God made us, and he knows how hard it can be for us to obey. That's one reason God gives us a Helper—the Holy Spirit. The Holy Spirit reminds us of what God wants us to do, then gives us the strength to do it. Let's see what good and bad things can happen when we choose to obey and disobey.**

TEACHER TIP

If you have adults in your class, this is a great time for children to realize that adults don't always get to do what they want to do!

Tumbling Pyramids

Set out scissors, glue sticks or transparent tape, and copies of the "Maybe, Maybe Not" section of the "Tumbling Pyramids" handout (p. 56). Have students cut on the solid lines, fold on the dotted lines, and fold the handout into a pyramid shape.

When everyone has a completed pyramid, have students line up across one end of the room facing you. Hold up a bag that contains treats. Say: **We're going to play a game similar to Mother, May I? When I call out a command, toss your pyramids in the air. You'll do whatever it says on the side of the pyramid that lands facing you. As soon as you reach me, you can have one of the treats in this bag. Ready? Here we go!**

Give a series of commands similar to these:

- **Shake hands with two people.**
- **Sing "Happy Birthday" as fast as you can.**
- **Smile and take a bow.**
- **Spin around three times.**
- **Pinch your nose and say, "I'm a very nice person."**
- **Pat yourself on the head.**
- **Touch your toes.**
- **Make a funny face.**
- **Croak like a frog.**
- **Do three shoulder rolls.**
- **Touch your nose.**

As you give commands, students will be moving forward or back, depending on how their pyramids land. As students reach you, give them treats and have them sit and watch the rest of the students play. Stop the game before students lose interest, then gather everyone in a circle.

Say: **Since some of you had trouble obeying, and since I'm such a nice person, I'll give you a treat anyway.** Ask:

- **Why did some of you disobey so often?** (Because of the way the pyramids landed.)

- **Why do people disobey in real life?** (They want to do things their way; they don't want to be told what to do.)

- **What were the consequences of disobeying?** (It took longer to get a treat; it was frustrating.)

- **What are the consequences when people disobey in real life?** (They sin and mess up their lives; bad things might happen to them.)

- **What does God want us to do after we've disobeyed?** (Say we're sorry; ask forgiveness, then start obeying.)

Say: **I have another pyramid for you to make. This pyramid shows how to obey God.**

Distribute the "Way to Obey" section of the "Tumbling Pyramids" handout and have students assemble it as before. As students work on their pyramids, ask:

● **What's one way you can listen to God this week?** (Stop and check in with God several times a day; listen to God before I get up in the morning.)

● **What's one way you can make a commitment to obey God this week?** (I can say, "God, I want to obey you"; I can put God first and put things I want to do second.)

● **Why is it important to pray for God's help?** (He can give us the power to obey; God can make us brave because we know he's with us.)

● **When do you know it's time to take action?** (When God gives me an opportunity; when God lets me know.)

Say: **When you get home, you might use a needle and thread to poke through the top of your "Way to Obey" pyramid and make a hanger. Hang it somewhere as a reminder that ★ God wants us to obey him. And remember, Jesus says that when we obey God, our joy will be full!**

CLOSING

Ready to Obey

Close with a prayer similar to this one: **Dear Lord, thank you for giving us opportunities to live for you and serve you. Help us listen to you every day and help us be ready to obey. Thank you for the joy that comes from obeying you. In Jesus' name, amen.**

TUMBLING PYRAMIDS

Cut out the pyramids on the solid lines, then crease them on the dotted lines.
Fold them into pyramid shapes and secure them with tape or glue.

MAYBE, MAYBE NOT

WAY TO OBEY

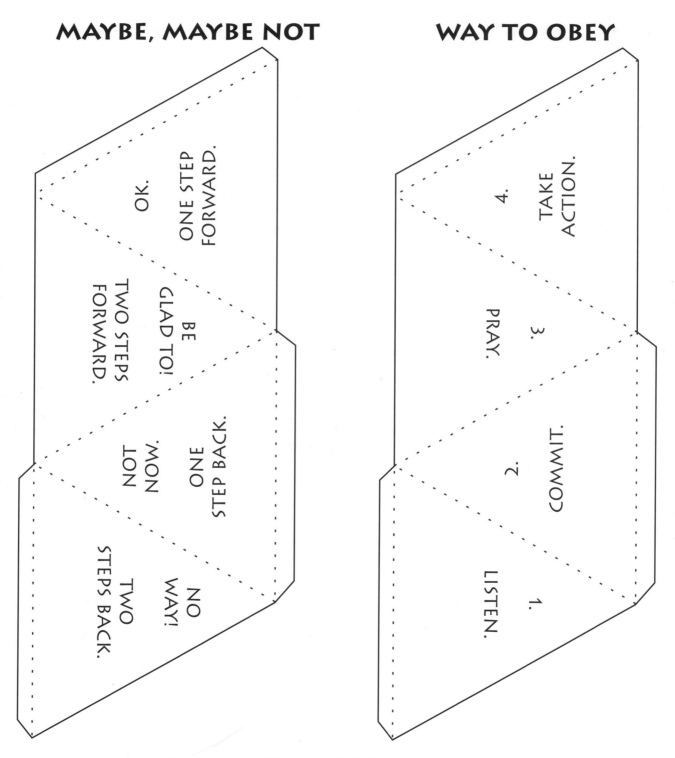

OK.

ONE STEP FORWARD.

TWO STEPS FORWARD.

BE GLAD TO!

NOT NOW.

ONE STEP BACK.

TWO STEPS BACK.

NO WAY!

4. TAKE ACTION.

3. PRAY.

2. COMMIT.

1. LISTEN.

A Little Man's Big Change

LESSON AIM

To help kids understand that ★ God is always ready to forgive us.

OBJECTIVES

Kids will
● experience unfairness in a game,
● discover why the people of Jericho disliked Zacchaeus,
● learn that love and forgiveness can melt bad feelings, and
● understand why it's important to forgive.

YOU'LL NEED

❑ a plastic tablecloth
❑ five containers of progressively larger sizes
❑ masking tape
❑ bags of jelly beans
❑ a quarter-cup measuring cup or scoop
❑ a roll of bathroom tissue or adding machine tape
❑ Bibles
❑ ice cubes
❑ photocopies of the "Heart of Forgiveness" handout (p. 65)
❑ scissors
❑ red and white construction paper

BIBLE BASIS

Luke 19:1-10

Zacchaeus was a guy everyone loved to hate. Not only did he collaborate with the hated Roman government as a tax collector, he was crooked to boot! Zacchaeus was the lowest of the low—a greedy villain who didn't care who suffered from his misdeeds. No wonder the crowd expressed shock and dismay when Jesus said, "Zacchaeus, hurry and come down! I must stay at your house today." Unthinkable! Outrageous! Jesus had really gone too far.

Or had he? Jesus always welcomed sinners who were somehow humbled and broken when confronted by his love. Jesus must've seen something the rest of us miss—the misery and despair of a life out of control, the potential for good, the desperate desire to change. Zacchaeus' change was both immediate and profound. He gave half his wealth to the poor and repaid his victims four times the amount he'd stolen from them.

There's an important lesson here for all Christians: God extends his grace and forgiveness to every man, woman, and child on this earth who approaches in humble repentance. Football has ineligible receivers. God doesn't.

Luke 6:37

In this passage, Jesus makes it clear that for Christians, a willingness to forgive is a requirement, not an option. And that's a tough assignment. If we set high standards of behavior for ourselves, it seems natural to have the same expectations of others. It's important to remember that our self-righteousness is "as filthy rags." God has forgiven our imperfections and we, in turn, must forgive others'.

UNDERSTANDING YOUR KIDS

Most kids—even many Christian kids—think it's OK to nurse a grudge. It seems to kids that friends and enemies just happen. If Katrina was rude to me today, I'll just be rude to her the rest of the week or the rest of the school year or the rest of my life. That's just the way things work out, right? Not!

Children often fail to realize that there's another side to every story. Maybe Katrina is feeling a lot of pressure from her parents to get good grades. Maybe her older sister bit her head off just before they left for school. Maybe Katrina's world is a dark, awful place right now, and the child in your class just happened to be the next person she bumped into.

Kids need to see that sometimes their perceptions about people can be off the mark. To the people of Jericho, Zacchaeus was a dastardly villain. To Jesus he was a miserable creature, desperately in need of compassion and forgiveness. This lesson will help your students respond with compassion to those who need their forgiveness and love.

ATTENTION GRABBER

The Lesson

Jelly Bean Scene

Spread a clean plastic tablecloth on the floor and set five clean containers of progressively larger sizes on it. Set the smallest container in the front and the largest in the back. For example, the smallest container might be a rinsed tin can, and the largest might be a clean bucket. Mark a starting line with masking tape about two feet from the first container. Leave several inches between containers so that the last container is about four feet behind the first.

As kids arrive, give them each a bag containing 15 jelly beans. Choose a confident child to be the "tax collector." Take the tax collector aside, give him or her a large bag of jelly beans, and explain that he or she is to move the starting line back about a foot after the first round, then about a yard after the second round. Explain that during the discussion time at the end of the game, you'll prompt him or her to take everyone's red jelly beans.

Say: **You'll take turns standing behind the starting line and tossing your jelly beans into the containers. The goal is to drop your first jelly bean into the first container, the second jelly bean into the second container, and so on. We'll play three rounds. You can collect all the jelly beans that go into the right containers. But the tax collector gets to keep all the jelly beans that miss. Ready? Let's play!**

Have kids take turns tossing five beans. Let each player collect the beans that land in the containers. Have the tax collector snatch away the beans that miss. After everyone's had a turn, prompt the tax collector to say, "This game is too easy! I'm gonna fix it," and move the starting line back a foot. After the second round, have the tax collector move the starting line back a yard. If the kids complain, simply play along and say: **I guess we'd better do what the tax collector says—he's** (she's) **in charge!**

After the third round, call everyone together and have kids show how many jelly beans they've collected. Have the tax collector show how many he or she has collected. Then ask:

59

● **How did you like this game?** (It was fun; it wasn't fair; it was too hard.)

● **Did you think it was fair when the tax collector moved the line? Why or why not?** (No, because it got harder and the tax collector got to keep more beans; no, it gave the tax collector an unfair advantage.)

Say: **Well, I'm sorry to say this, but I think our tax collector has even more bad news.** Prompt the tax collector to demand and collect everyone's red jelly beans. Then call the tax collector over to you. Say: **These kids seem pretty upset with the way this game turned out. You've got a lot more jelly beans than anyone else.** Hand the tax collector a quarter-cup measuring cup or scoop and say: **We don't want to make any enemies, so I'll help you give everyone a nice big scoop of jelly beans.**

After you've added jelly beans to each student's bag, say: **Today we're going to discover that ★ God is always ready to forgive us—even when we take other people's jelly beans! What happened in our game is a lot like what happens in our Bible story today. Let's set our jelly bean bags over by the wall and see what happens to the nasty, cheating, mean, greedy tax collector in our story.**

Be sure to reserve some jelly beans for the "Hearts of Forgiveness" activity.

BIBLE STUDY

Tax-to-the-Max Zack (Luke 19:1-10)

Say: **First, let's set the stage for our story. At the far end of the room we need to make a tree by having two students stand on either side of a chair.** Have two volunteers stand on either side of a chair, holding their arms out like branches. Coach them to help "Zacchaeus" (za-KEE-us) climb safely on the chair and back down again during the story. **Now we need someone to play Jesus and stand at the opposite end of the room from the tree. Next we need a person to play Zacchaeus and stand between the tree and Jesus. Zacchaeus was a little guy, so you'll need to get down on your knees.** Position the actors playing Jesus and Zacchaeus. **The rest of you will be the crowd. Stand here near the middle of the road in front of Zacchaeus. Good! You folks in the crowd don't like Zack, so every time I mention his name, you can boo. But you love Jesus, so every time I mention his name, you can clap and cheer. I'll be the narrator. Here we go!**

Read the story "Tax-to-the-Max Zack" (p. 61), pausing to coach the actors.

After the story, have kids give themselves a big round of

Tax-to-the-Max Zack

(based on Luke 19:1-10)

Long ago, in Jesus' time, there lived a man we'll call Tax-to-the-Max Zack. Zack worked for the hated Roman government—that made him a traitor. He was their chief tax collector—that made him really unpopular. And he was as crooked as a cow's hind leg. He always added a little to everyone's tax bill and kept the extra for himself—that made him a cheat. Why, Zack would even cheat a blind widow. This guy was the lowest of the low.

One day the people of Jericho (that's where Zack lived) heard that Jesus was coming to town. The town fairly burst with excitement. Everyone jabbered about Jesus. "I wonder if he'll do a miracle," said some. "I hope he heals my grandmother," said another. "She's been sick for such a long time."

Long before Jesus appeared, a big crowd started to form along the road. Zack was there too, but he got pushed clear to the back. No one was about to make room for Tax-to-the-Max. No sirree. Jesus wouldn't want to get near him anyway—or so everyone thought.

Finally the people could see Jesus walking down the road toward Jericho. Everyone strained to get a look. But Zack was stuck in the back and, being a little guy, couldn't see a thing. Then he noticed a tree just a little way up the road. "I could climb that tree," Zack thought. "Then I could see Jesus too."

So Zack climbed the tree. "Oh, good!" he thought. "Now I can see Jesus. And he's coming right this way!"

Zack's heart started beating ker-thump, ker-thump, ker-thump! Jesus headed straight for the sycamore tree where Zack was perched. Jesus looked up and said, "Zacchaeus, hurry and come down! I must stay at your house today."

Everyone in the crowd gasped. Even Zack could hardly believe his ears. Jesus wanted to visit *him?* The crowd began to mumble and complain. "Doesn't Jesus know this man is a sinner? Why would the Lord want to visit Tax-to-the-Max?"

But that's just what Jesus did. And you'd never believe what happened to Zack. He changed—just like that! Jesus' love crept into that mean, nasty heart of his. Jesus must've seen something in Zack that no one else could see. Jesus saw that Zack was sorry for all the wrong things he'd done and all the people he'd hurt. Jesus saw that Zack wanted to be forgiven so he could have a clean heart and new life. Why, Zack stood right up and said to Jesus, "I will give half of my possessions to the poor. And if I have cheated anyone, I will pay back four times more."

A big smile crossed Jesus' face, and he said, "Salvation has come to this house today, because this man also belongs to the family of Abraham. The Son of Man came to find lost people and save them."

Well, if Jesus could save Zack, he could save anyone.

applause. Then gather everyone and ask:

● **Why was Zack so unpopular?** (Because he cheated; because he took people's money; because he worked for the Romans.)

● **Do you blame the people of Jericho for feeling the way they did about Zack? Explain.** (No, because he was a rotten guy; no, I probably would have disliked him too.)

● **If you'd been in Jericho that day, how would you have reacted when Jesus announced that he wanted to visit Zack's house?** (I probably would have been surprised; I probably wouldn't have liked it; I might have gotten mad at Jesus.)

● **Why do you think Jesus announced in front of the whole crowd that he wanted to go to Zack's house?** (He wanted people to see that he loved everyone; people needed to know that God can forgive everyone.)

● **Why do you think visiting with Jesus made such a big change in Zack's life?** (Because he could feel Jesus' love; because he wanted to be like Jesus and be one of Jesus' followers.)

● **What can we learn from the story of Zacchaeus?** (That God loves everyone; that God can forgive anybody; that we should realize that bad people sometimes want to change.)

Say: **The people of Jericho probably thought that Zack was rich and happy. But in reality, Zack was rich and miserable. Zack had heard about Jesus' miracles and must have had faith that Jesus could change even his miserable, rotten life. Zack and the people of Jericho learned that ★ God is always ready to forgive us. Let's see what other lessons we can discover from this story.**

LIFE APPLICATION

Wrapped Up and Frozen
Have the child who played Zacchaeus stand in the middle of the class. Have the rest of the kids make a circle around Zacchaeus and begin wrapping him or her with bathroom tissue or adding machine tape.

Say: **We want to wrap Zacchaeus from head to toe to show that Zacchaeus was all wrapped up in sin.** Ask:

● **How does sin wrap you up?** (When you do something wrong, you usually have to do something else wrong to cover it up; when you do bad things, people blame you for other things.)

Say: **Pretty soon Zacchaeus was wrapped up by hate, too, because no one liked him. If Zacchaeus had dropped dead, people would probably have cheered. But Jesus was different. Jesus saw how much Zacchaeus was hurting inside. And Jesus wanted to set him free.** Ask:

● **How could Zacchaeus be set free from his sin?** (By asking forgiveness; by telling Jesus he was sorry.)

Say: **Listen to what the Bible says about forgiveness.** Have a volunteer read 1 John 1:9 aloud. Then say: **God is the only one who can truly set us free from sin, and ★ God is always ready to forgive us. All we have to do is ask. Zacchaeus, I think it's time for you to break out!** Have everyone help the student playing Zacchaeus burst out of the paper that's holding him or her. Say, "Yes!" and lead the class in a round of applause. Then ask Zacchaeus:

● **How did it feel, being all wrapped up?** (Tight; bad.)

● **What was it like to break out?** (Cool; it felt good.)

● **How do you think the real Zacchaeus felt when his sins were forgiven?** (Free; like a new person; clean.)

● **How do you think the people in Jericho felt when they saw what had happened to Zacchaeus?** (Some were probably happy; others might have doubted that it was for real.)

Say: **It isn't always easy to forgive, especially if a person has hurt us in some way.** Have kids form pairs. Give each pair a small ice cube. **Unforgiveness freezes the flow of God's love. Jesus warned us about that. As I read Jesus' words, see how quickly you and your partner can melt your ice cube. You can take turns holding it so no one's hands get too cold.**

As pairs work on melting their ice cubes, read the following passages from an easy-to-understand version of the Bible: Matthew 6:13-15; Luke 6:37; and Colossians 3:13.

As the ice cubes continue to melt, ask:

● **What did you learn from these Scriptures?** (That we need to forgive others if we want God to forgive us; that if we don't forgive other people, God won't forgive us.)

● **How is melting an ice cube like forgiving someone?** (It melts away bad feelings; it helps people feel warm toward each other.)

● **Why should we forgive people who've done bad things?** (Because God is willing to forgive them; because God still loves them, and we should too.)

Say: **Sometimes we need to ask God to help us see people through Jesus' eyes—through eyes of love. Jesus helped the people of Jericho see the change in Zacchaeus, and he can do the same for us today.**

COMMITMENT

Hearts of Forgiveness

Say: **Let's make something to remind us that forgiveness is a gift from God, a gift that God wants us to pass on to others.**

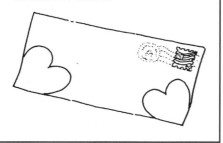
Distribute photocopies of the "Heart of Forgiveness" handout (p. 65), scissors, and red and white construction paper. Demonstrate how to use the pattern to cut the red and white paper and how to weave the basket.

As students work, discuss the topic of forgiveness. Ask questions such as "When is it really hard to forgive someone?" and "How do you feel after you've asked God for forgiveness?"

Have kids sit in a circle with their completed heart baskets in hand. Bring the remaining jelly beans and join kids in the circle. Say: ★ **God is always ready to forgive us, and God expects us to pass his forgiveness along to others.**

Turn to the student on your right, pour a few jelly beans in his or her heart basket, then say: (Name)**, God is always ready to forgive you.** Pass the bag of jelly beans to that student and have him or her repeat the process with the next student. Continue until each person has been affirmed.

Say: **Forgiving people who have hurt us is one of the hardest things God asks us to do. I'd like you to close your eyes and take a few quiet moments to think about someone you've had difficulty forgiving. You may want to ask God to help you see that person through Jesus' eyes.** Pause for a few moments. **Keeping your eyes closed, eat one of the jelly beans from your basket. Let that jelly bean represent how God has forgiven you. Now eat another jelly bean to represent the forgiveness that you can pass on to others.**

CLOSING

Full Hearts

Say: **Now you may open your eyes. You'll notice that we started this activity by filling each other's baskets. That's important because God doesn't expect us to forgive from an empty heart. First God fills our hearts with his love and forgiveness, then he asks us to pass that love and forgiveness on to others.**

Have kids stand for prayer. Close with a prayer similar to this one: **Lord, thank you that ★ you're always ready to forgive us. Help us learn to see people through your eyes and to pass your love and forgiveness on to others. In Jesus' name, amen.**

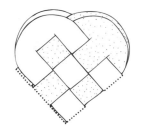

Heart of Forgiveness

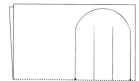
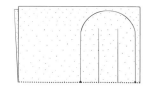

1 Cut the pattern from red construction paper and white construction paper.

2 Lay the red and white patterns side by side, curved ends up.

3 Weave the inside red strip through the inside white strip, around the center white strip, and through the outside white strip. Push the red strip up.

4 Weave the center red strip around the inside white strip, through the center white strip, and around the outside white strip.

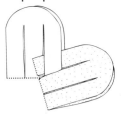

5 Weave the outside red strip through the inside white strip, around the center white strip, and through the outside white strip. When the basket is finished, it will resemble a woven, heart-shaped pocket.

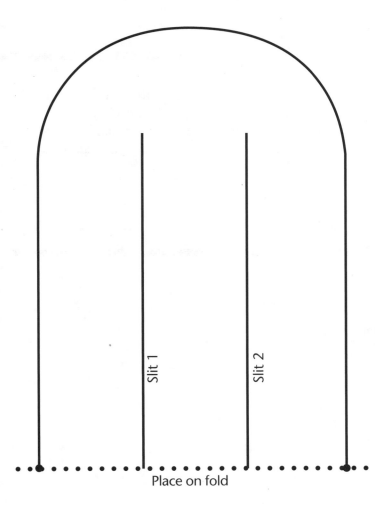

Slit 1

Slit 2

Place on fold

6 Family Circles

LESSON AIM

To help kids understand that ★ Jesus cares about our families.

OBJECTIVES

Kids or families will
● hear how Jesus helped Jairus and his little girl,
● discover how family members depend on each other,
● make affirmation cards for members of their families, and
● reflect upon the need to show love and appreciation to each member of their families.

NOTE

This lesson works well with an intergenerational class. You may wish to invite whole families to join you for this session.

YOU'LL NEED

❑ balloons
❑ masking tape
❑ large potatoes
❑ bowls of water
❑ bars of soap
❑ paper towels
❑ safety pins
❑ sandwich bags
❑ tablespoons
❑ a bowl of peanuts
❑ a bowl of M&M's
❑ a bowl of raisins
❑ Bibles
❑ scissors
❑ markers or colored pencils

❏ photocopies of the "From the Bottom of My Heart" handout (p. 75)
❏ photocopies of the "Thanks a Bunch" handout (p. 76)

BIBLE BASIS

Mark 5:21-24, 35-43

Desperation drove Jairus to Jesus. Jairus' daughter lay dying and his only hope was in the healing hands of the controversial teacher from Nazareth. What a juicy tidbit of gossip Jairus must have generated when he pushed his way through a crowd and fell at Jesus' feet with half the population of Capernaum looking on! Nicodemus, another teacher, had dared to come to Jesus only by night. Would Jairus lose his position as a synagogue leader? Who would leak the word to his superiors in Jerusalem?

I have the feeling that Jairus cared nothing for the crowd's opinion or for whatever the consequences of his actions might be. Jairus had only one thing on his mind: his daughter's life. There was an almost tangible sense of relief when Jesus started toward Jairus' house. But then Jesus stopped to address a woman who had touched his cloak and been healed. Jesus turned to see who had touched him, commended her faith, and affirmed her healing. There stood Jairus, thinking, "We've got to hurry!" And sure enough, before they started on their way again, a messenger came with the news that the little girl had died. But Jesus said to Jairus, "Don't be afraid; just believe."

Arriving at the home of Jairus, Jesus drove away the wailing mourners, entered with three disciples and the parents, took the dead girl's hand, and said, "Young girl, I tell you to stand up!" And she did. The master of life and death had compassion for a grieving family and gave them back their child. Families form the very core of God's plan for his people. Jesus cares for the families represented by your students every bit as much as he cared for the family of Jairus.

Colossians 3:12-21

Being a member of a loving family is *work!* While we look to the interests of others, we need to be ready to forgive quickly when our own wants and needs get less than top priority. It's unrealistic to say there should never be spats and hurt feelings, but it's quite realistic to expect loving communication and freely given forgiveness.

UNDERSTANDING YOUR KIDS

Teaching a lesson on families is always tricky because you can't be sure what kinds of family-related trauma your students may be facing. Single-parent and blended families are nearly as common in the church as in society at large.

Because children tend to blame themselves for whatever goes wrong in their families, it's important for each child to come away from this lesson with the clear understanding that his or her family is important to God, no matter what that family looks like. The Bible is full of stories about imperfect families. Use this lesson to help kids understand that they can serve God by showing respect, love, and care for each member of their families.

The Lesson ATTENTION GRABBER

Baby Boom

As students arrive, assign them to teams of four, keeping even numbers of younger and older children or adults on each team. If the number of people in your class isn't evenly divisible by four, ask for volunteers to be helpers. Give each team member an uninflated balloon. Place a long strip of masking tape down one side of the room, about five feet from a wall. Have teams stand behind that line. Have helpers place the following items by the wall opposite each team: a large potato, a bowl of water, a bar of soap, two paper towels, and a safety pin.

Say: **We're going to start our lesson on families today with a wild and crazy baby boom relay. When I say "go," blow up and tie off your balloon as quickly as you can. You can help your teammates—it's OK if your "stronger windbags" blow up all the balloons. Once your balloons are tied off, drop them on the floor and "hatch" them by sitting on them and popping them. When your team has hatched all its balloons, you and your teammates will take turns running to the opposite wall to do these four tasks:**

● **Use soap, water, and a paper towel to wash and dry the potato "baby."**

● **Pin a paper towel "diaper" on the potato baby.**

● **Rock the baby and sing one verse of "Jesus Loves Me."**

● **Toss the baby back to the rest of the team.**

I'll give you a minute to decide which team member will

do each task. You all have to participate. My helpers will make sure you perform each task carefully and completely.

Give teams a few moments to decide which teammate will do each task. Review the directions and assure students that you'll call out the directions during the game.

When the teams have organized themselves, say "go!" Keep a close watch on each team's progress and be ready to prompt teams on their next task. If helpers think that a team hasn't properly cared for its potato baby, they can call a team member back to repeat the task. When all the potato babies have been cared for and tossed to team members behind the line, have students give themselves a round of applause.

Then say: **Sit in a circle with your teammates and your potato baby and discuss these questions:**

● **How was working together in this game like how families work together?** (They have to take turns taking care of little children; families are in a hurry most of the time; caring for babies is hard work.)

● **How was it different?** (You wouldn't throw a real baby; in families parents usually do more work than children.)

● **What are some things you remember about being a teeny-tiny child?** (I remember a rocking horse; I remember blowing out birthday candles; I remember getting a puppy.)

Call everyone together and invite groups to share what they learned in their discussions.

Say: **It takes lots of work to raise a child. When you were little, your parents had to watch over you constantly. They fed you and changed you in the middle of the night—even when they were so sleepy they could hardly stand up! God puts us in families because he knows that we all need that special love and care that a family gives. Today we're going to learn that ★ Jesus cares about our families.**

BIBLE STUDY

Jairus Visits (Mark 5:21-24, 35-43)

You may want to ask a teenager or adult to visit your classroom in Bible costume as Jairus and tell the story "A Desperate Father" (p. 70). Or, if you have parents in your class, ask for a volunteer to slip on a Bible costume and read the story.

Say: **I've asked a special visitor to come to our class today and tell us how Jesus helped his family. Let's welcome Jairus!**

Have "Jairus" shake hands with the children and ask their names. Then have him gather everyone in a circle on the floor to

A Desperate Father

(based on Mark 5:21-24, 35-43)

Good morning! When I heard that you were learning that ★ Jesus cares about our families, I just had to visit your class. You see, Jesus did something for my family that I'll never, ever forget.

My name is Jairus, and I'm a leader of the synagogue in the city of Capernaum. A synagogue is like a Jewish church. People come to the synagogue to worship God, pray, listen to the priests, and read from the Scriptures.

When we heard that Jesus was coming to our town, everyone was excited. Well, almost everyone. Some of the Jewish leaders here and in Jerusalem think Jesus is a fake. I don't agree. No one but the Son of God could do the miracles Jesus does! But I've learned to keep quiet about my opinions so that I don't get in trouble.

My story is about my daughter. She's a 12-year-old bundle of energy and laughter and love! One night my wife heard our daughter cry out in her sleep. She got up to see what was wrong, then came running back to me.

"Jairus! Jairus!" she cried, shaking my shoulder. "Our daughter is burning up with fever! I don't know what's wrong—what shall we do?"

We sat by her bed the rest of the night, but there was nothing we could do to help her. By morning she didn't even know who we were. A hard lump of fear knotted in my chest.

"She's going to die, isn't she?" my wife asked.

Just then I heard some of our neighbors out in the street. "Come down to the lake," they shouted to anyone who would listen. "Jesus, the teacher from Nazareth, is there."

"If anyone can help our daughter, Jesus can," I told my wife excitedly. "If I could just get him to come here . . ."

"Hurry then, Jairus," my wife urged. "Go quickly! You must get him to come before it's too late."

I found Jesus in the middle of a huge crowd of people. "Let me through!" I cried, but everyone wanted to be close to Jesus. I pushed and shoved until I finally got through. Then I fell at Jesus' feet.

"My little daughter is dying! Please come and put your hands on her so that she will be healed and live," I begged.

Jesus agreed to come. "We must hurry!" I urged. But then a woman touched Jesus' cloak and was healed. When Jesus stopped to talk to her, I almost panicked. Then I felt one of my servants tugging at my sleeve.

"Your daughter is dead," he said. "Why bother the teacher anymore?"

Before I could respond, Jesus looked me straight in the eye. "Don't be afraid," he said. "Just believe."

I tried to believe—what else could I do? When we arrived at my house, Jesus asked the mourners, "Why are you crying and making so much noise? The child is not dead, only asleep."

Some people laughed at Jesus, but I kept on praying he was right. He went to the bed where she lay all white and still. He took her hand and commanded, "Young girl, I tell you to stand up!" And she stood up, ran to my wife and me, and gave us a big hug.

Jesus smiled at us as we stood there hugging and crying. He gently reminded us to give our daughter something to eat, then he left. I'll never forget that day. I learned that Jesus really does care about families, and not only families in Bible times. Jesus cares about your family, too.

hear his story.

After the story, have everyone give Jairus a round of applause. Then ask:

● **Do you think it was easy or hard for Jairus to ask Jesus for help?** (Easy, because he was afraid his daughter would die; hard, because he might get in trouble with the other Jewish leaders and lose his job.)

● **How did Jairus feel when he had to push through the crowd to get to Jesus?** (Scared that he'd be too late; afraid that Jesus might not come in time.)

● **Why did Jesus agree to go with Jairus when he was already talking to a whole crowd of people?** (Because he knew how much Jairus loved his daughter; because Jairus had lots of faith; because he cared about Jairus' family.)

Say: ★ **Jesus cares about our families today, just as he cared for Jairus' family long ago. Let's have some fun discovering more of what the Bible has to say about families.**

LIFE APPLICATION

Countin' on You!

Have students rejoin their groups of four. Have the extra people who were helpers during the Attention Grabber join other groups—it's OK to have groups of different sizes.

Say: **In your group, decide who will be the mom, who will be the dad, who will be a big kid, and who will be a little kid. It's OK to have more than one big kid or little kid.**

While groups are assigning their roles, set on a table sandwich bags; several tablespoons; and bowls of peanuts, M&M's, and raisins.

Say: **When I call out "dads," I want all the dads to pop up and take turns telling what families count on dads to do. When you've named all the things you can think of, I'll tell you what to do next. Then we'll repeat the game with all the other family members. When we're finished, you'll have a delicious treat to enjoy. Here we go. Dads!**

Have all the dads pop up and take turns telling what families count on dads to do. Students might mention taking care of the car, mowing the lawn, cooking on the grill, bringing home a paycheck, talking through problems, or helping with schoolwork.

After the dads have named all the responsibilities they can think of, say: **OK, dads, run to the table and take a sandwich bag to everyone in your group.**

Then call out "moms." Students may mention planning birthday parties, getting groceries, planning meals, bringing home a pay-

TEACHER TIP

Be open to all of the suggestions, even if they don't conform to traditional roles.

check, taking care of people when they're sick, tucking children in at night, or taking kids to music lessons. When students have named all the responsibilities they can think of, have the moms run back and forth between the table and their groups, putting a spoonful of raisins in each person's bag.

Next call out, "big kids." Students may mention taking out the garbage, feeding the pets, helping with dishes, mowing the lawn, baby-sitting, or running errands. When students have named all the responsibilities they can think of, have the big kids run back and forth between the table and their groups, putting a spoonful of peanuts in each person's bag.

Finally call out, "little kids." Students may mention such things as giving hugs, telling jokes, bringing joy and laughter, picking up toys, and obeying parents. When students have named all the things they can think of, have the little kids run back and forth between the table and their groups, putting a spoonful of M&M's in each person's bag.

Encourage students to enjoy their treats as they discuss these questions in their groups:

● **What did we gain by working together as a family in this activity?** (We got a good treat; food!)

● **What do we gain by working together in our real families?** (A happy home; good feelings; love for each other.)

● **Why do you think God put us in families?** (So we can care for each other; so we'll have people who love us.)

Invite students to share what they learned from their discussions.

Then say: **In families, we count on each other for lots of things. And that's why God put us in families. Not all families look alike, so sometimes we count on each other for different things. Listen to what the Bible says about how important it is to take care of each other in our families.** Have a volunteer look up and read 1 Timothy 5:8.

Say: **The Bible tells us that taking care of each other in our families is one of the most important things we can do. God put us in families so we would have people to love us and take care of us. That's why ★ Jesus cares about our families.**

COMMITMENT

Thanks to You!

Say: **When you put people together under the same roof day after day and year after year, things won't always be perfect! We all get the crabbies and grouchies, and when we do, the other people in our families had better watch out! Let's find** out more about what the Bible says people should do to build loving, happy families.

Distribute Bibles to each group. Assign half of the groups Colossians 3:12-14. Assign the other groups Colossians 3:15-21. Have groups search their passages for God's instructions for families. Allow two or three minutes for study, then call everyone together and ask groups to report what they discovered.

Say: **Turn to a partner and discuss these questions:**

● **Which of these instructions is hardest for you to follow?** (Obeying parents; being thankful when things aren't going well.)

● **How can you do better in that area?** (I can ask God to remind me; by thinking of others instead of just thinking of myself.)

Say: **I know there's one thing we can all do better. When we count on people for the same thing day after day, it's easy to forget to say thank you. So today we're going to take time to make thank you notes for the people in our families.**

Set out scissors, markers or colored pencils, and photocopies of the "From the Bottom of My Heart" and "Thanks a Bunch" handouts (pp. 75-76). Encourage students to make cards for people in their families who would appreciate a special thank you. Have kids decorate their cards and fill in the names of the people who'll receive them. Then demonstrate how to fold and cut each card.

1. Cut around the border of each card.

2. Fold each card in half the long way.

3. Cut the heart from the top center to the upper dots, then from the bottom center to the lower dots.

4. Cut the "Thanks a Bunch" banner from the top center to the upper dots and from the center dot below the carrots to the banner.

5. Fold each card in half the other way.

6. Pull the center of each card forward and fold it as you close the card so the design will pop up when the card is opened.

As students create their cards, circulate and ask questions such as "What's one really happy time you remember sharing with your family?" and "What do you like best about your family?"

As time for working on the cards draws to a close, give two-minute and one-minute warnings. Then gather everyone for the closing activity.

CLOSING

Circles of Love

Have students set their cards aside then stand in circles in their groups of four and hold hands. If you've invited parents for today's lesson, have families stand together in a circle.

Say: **Listen and follow my instructions carefully.** Give these instructions in a spirit of quiet reflection, pausing for a moment after each one. Say:

● **If you've ever failed to say thank you when someone in your family did something nice for you, drop your hands and close your eyes.**

● **If you've ever lost your temper and shouted at a family member, turn around and face away from your circle.**

● **If you've ever complained to an outsider about someone in your family, take a step away from your circle.**

● **If you've ever hurt the feelings of someone in your family, take another step away.**

● **If you've ever tried to encourage someone in your family, turn around.**

● **If you've ever helped take care of a family member who was sick, take a step toward your circle.**

● **If you've ever given up your plans to do what another family member wanted to do, take another step toward your circle.**

● **If you've ever forgiven a family member who hurt your feelings, open your eyes and put your arms around the people on either side of you.**

Say: **Please remain in your circles as I close in prayer.** Pray: **Dear Lord, thank you for caring about our families. Remind us this week to show love and appreciation to each member of our families. Help us to be slow to get angry and quick to forgive. In Jesus' name, amen.**

from the bottom of my heart!

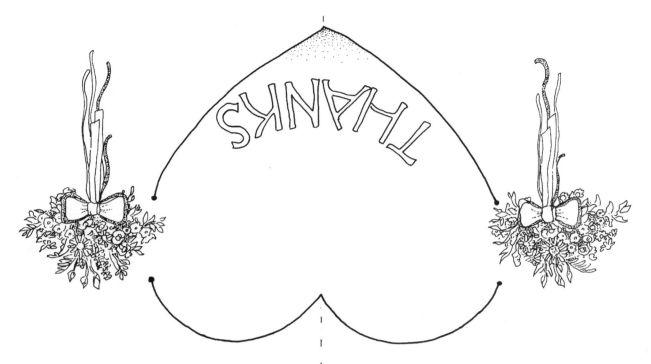

THANKS

DEAR

For all the things
you do each day,
It makes me very
glad to say...

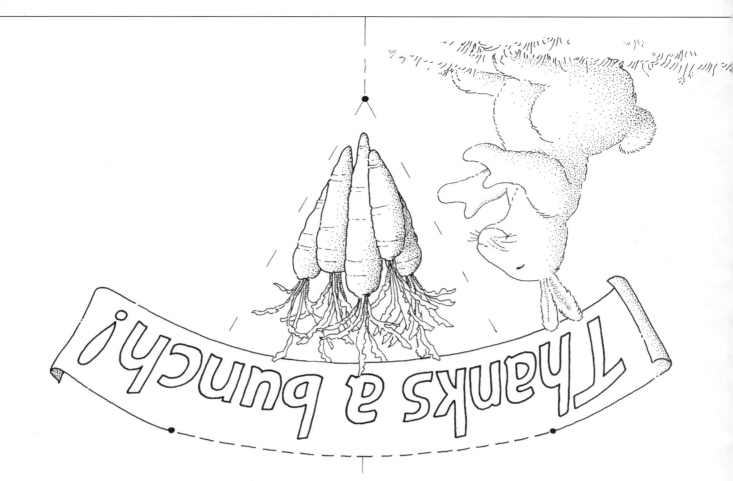

Thanks a bunch!

YOU'RE the world's BEST

I have a hunch,
So I want to say...

Sowing and Growing

LESSON AIM

To help kids understand that ★ Jesus wants us to tell others about him.

OBJECTIVES

Kids will
- act out the parable of the sower,
- learn how they can "sow" God's Word,
- understand why it's important to tell others about Jesus, and
- practice sharing their faith.

YOU'LL NEED

- ❑ grape soda
- ❑ vanilla ice cream
- ❑ a blindfold
- ❑ an ice-cream scoop
- ❑ cups
- ❑ spoons
- ❑ Bibles
- ❑ a photocopy of the "Parable of the Sower" script (pp. 81-82)
- ❑ scissors
- ❑ photocopies of the "Dough-n't You Know God Loves You?" handout (p. 86)
- ❑ peanut butter
- ❑ powdered sugar
- ❑ plastic sandwich bags
- ❑ photocopies of the "God's Garden" handout (p. 87)

❏ tacks or transparent tape
❏ colored pencils or markers

BIBLE BASIS

Matthew 13:3-9, 18-23

Jesus, being a wise teacher, related deep truths about God's kingdom through simple stories about agrarian life that his listeners could readily understand. Compared to the endless arguing and nit-picking of the scribes, Pharisees, and Sadducees, Jesus' teaching must have seemed lively, relevant, and fresh. The parable of the sower is such a story.

Even his own disciples asked Jesus why he taught in parables. Jesus explained that understanding would be given only to those who had faith. Critics who listened intending to argue and contradict would find little in Jesus' simple anecdotes to criticize. But those who listened with faith would discover profound truths and insights about God's kingdom. We can interpret all of Jesus' parables at many different levels. In this lesson we'll focus on the idea that kids can be sowers and that when they share their faith, they can trust God to produce fruit for his kingdom.

1 Corinthians 2:9

God has unimaginably wonderful things planned for us! To a child, Walt Disney World might qualify as unimaginably wonderful. But God is the mastermind of our glorious future. The label "child of God" carries with it incredible benefits. God gave us this good news to share with a world of lost people. Let's do it!

UNDERSTANDING YOUR KIDS

Young children are not at all shy about sharing their faith. If Laura's family honors Jesus as Lord, Laura naturally assumes that others will do the same. But as their social contacts increase, children become aware that not everyone accepts God's Word and that a large and vocal part of our society looks down on Christianity, labeling it simplistic and narrow-minded. It takes only one or two encounters with skeptics to make kids fearful of speaking out about their faith. Kids need to see that telling others about Jesus is like giving a precious gift. Use this lesson to help kids learn fun, practical, positive ways to share their faith.

The Lesson

Glob Tag

As students arrive, ask if they've ever seen a purple cow, then promise to show them one in class today. Set out chilled grape soda and vanilla ice cream. Explain that a purple cow is a float made with these ingredients and that kids will be able to sample one as soon as they've played the opening game.

Ask for a volunteer to be "It" for a game of Glob Tag. As you blindfold It, say: **The rest of you spread out around the room. Once I say "freeze" you can't move until It touches you. Then you'll hook arms with It and go in search of another person. You'll keep adding people until everyone is part of the "glob." Once you've joined the glob, you have to be silent. You can't tell It where to go or pull It in any direction—members of the glob just move along wherever It takes them. The game is over when everyone is part of the glob.**

Start the game by calling out: **Freeze!** Kids are likely to call to It to find them so they can finish the game and enjoy the treat you've promised. It's fine for kids to give verbal clues before they're caught, but remind them to stay silent after they've joined the glob. Be sure to guard the safety of the blindfolded person.

When everyone has been caught, remove Its blindfold and have everyone give him or her a round of applause.

Then have kids gather around a table and help you scoop ice cream into cups. As you pour grape soda over the ice cream and distribute spoons and the purple cows, ask:

● **What did you think about that game?** (I wanted to get it over with so we could have our treat; it was fun being part of the glob; I wanted to hurry up and get caught.)

● **What was good about being caught in Glob Tag?** (We got to be part of the glob; we wanted to hurry up and get the game over with so we could get our treats.)

Say: **Today we're going to learn that ★ Jesus wants us to tell others about him. We'll also discover some fun ways to help the kingdom of God grow. Jesus often told stories that started with the words, "The kingdom of heaven is like . . . " Well, I'd like to tell you that the kingdom of heaven is like a purple cow.** Take a cup from a student who has drunk all the grape soda but still has some ice cream left. **When I pour in this much soda** (indicate just an inch or two)**, the purple cow grows this much** (indicate twice the volume of the soda)**. In God's kingdom, when we put this much effort into telling others about Jesus** (indicate just an inch)**, God**

TEACHER TIP

An excellent way to see if kids understand the rules of a game is to ask them to explain the rules to you.

can take what we've done and make his kingdom grow **this much** (indicate twice the volume) **or even more. Jesus explained this in a special story we call the parable of the sower. As soon as you're finished slurping your purple cows, we'll present this Bible story in a way I guarantee you've never done before.**

Have kids help you gather the empty cups and used spoons.

BIBLE STUDY

Scripture in a Circle (Matthew 13:1-9, 18-23)

Designate an open area of your room as the "stage." To the left of the stage, have kids form a line that trails around the room in a circle. Choose an older child or adult to read the passages from Matthew phrase by phrase as students perform. You will be the stage manager. You'll call one, two, or three children to the stage and help them act out what's being read.

Say: **You're going to be the actors in our unique presentation of the parable of the sower. As our reader reads Jesus' words from the Bible, I'll call you up to the stage and tell you what to do. Then you'll scamper off the stage, rejoin the line, and watch the drama until it's your turn to perform again. Is everybody ready? Here we go!**

Give the reader a photocopy of the "Parable of the Sower" script (pp. 81-82) and signal him or her to begin.

If you have time, run through the Bible story drama again. It will go much more quickly than the first time, and the repetition will reinforce the story in kids' minds. Then gather everyone in a circle on the floor and ask:

● **What was this story about?** (A farmer; some seeds; God's kingdom.)

● **In this story, what does the farmer stand for?** (Someone who tells others about God; a Christian.)

● **What is the seed?** (God's Word; the gospel; the story of Jesus.)

● **How can we "produce fruit" for God's kingdom?** (By helping other people believe in Jesus; by telling people about God and the Bible.)

● **Who can be like the farmer and plant the seeds of God's Word in people's lives?** (Anyone; Christians; people who love God.)

Say: ★ **Jesus wants us to tell others about him. And when we do, we can trust God to help those seeds grow. When other people start believing in Jesus because of seeds we've helped to plant in their lives, that's how we**

Parable of the Sower

(Matthew 13:3-9, 18-23)

3 Then Jesus used stories to teach them many things. He said: "A farmer went out to plant his seed.

Have a "farmer" pretend to scatter seed then walk off.

4 While he was planting, some seed fell by the road, and the birds came and ate it all up.

Have two "seeds" curl up in a squatting position.
Have two "birds" swoop down on the seeds and carry them away.

5 Some seed fell on rocky ground, where there wasn't much dirt. That seed grew very fast, because the ground was not deep.

Have two seeds curl up in a squatting position then extend their arms and grow.

6 But when the sun rose, the plants dried up, because they did not have deep roots.

Have a big, scary "sun" tower over the seeds then run off with them.

7 Some other seed fell among thorny weeds, which grew and choked the good plants.

Have two seeds curl up in a squatting position then extend their arms and grow. Have two big, scary "weeds" pretend to choke the seeds then run off with them.

8 Some other seed fell on good ground where it grew and produced a crop. Some plants made thirty times more, some made sixty times more, and some made a hundred times more.*

Have three seeds curl up in a squatting position then extend their arms and "grow." Have the first seed grow a little, the second a little more, and the third as tall as possible.

9 You people who can hear me, listen.

Call all the children on stage and have them cup their hands around their ears.

18 So listen to the meaning of that story about the farmer.

Have children continue to cup their hands around their ears.

19 What is the seed that fell by the road?

Send all the children back to the line.

That seed is like the person who hears the message about the kingdom but does not understand it.

Have a seed curl up in a squatting position then stretch its arms and grow.

(continued)

81

The Evil One comes and takes away what was planted in that person's heart.

Have an older child swoop down on the seed and carry it away.

20 And what is the seed that fell on rocky ground? That seed is like the person who hears the teaching and quickly accepts it with joy.

Have a seed curl up in a squatting position, extend its arms and grow, then jump up and down with joy.

21 But he does not let the teaching go deep into his life, so he keeps it only a short time. When trouble or persecution comes because of the teaching he accepted, he quickly gives up.

Have the seed look scared, then have an older child swoop down on the seed and carry it away.

22 And what is the seed that fell among the thorny weeds? That seed is like the person who hears the teaching but lets worries about this life and the temptation of wealth stop that teaching from growing. So the teaching does not produce fruit in that person's life.

Have a seed curl up in a squatting position, extend its arms and grow, then look worried. Have an older child pretend to choke the seed then carry it away.

23 But what is the seed that fell on the good ground? That seed is like the person who hears the teaching and understands it. That person grows and produces fruit, sometimes thirty times more,

Send one-third of the children onto the stage. Have them sit down, cup their hands around their ears, nod their heads, then stretch out their arms.

sometimes sixty times more,

Send another third of the children onto the stage behind the children who are sitting. Have them kneel then stretch out their arms.

and sometimes a hundred times more."*

Send the rest of the children onto the stage and have them stand behind the first two rows then stretch their arms over their heads.

*The order of these numbers has been reversed intentionally.

produce fruit. We plant the seeds, and God makes those seeds bear fruit in the lives of other people. Let's find out what good things happen to people when they believe in Jesus.

Help children quickly form four groups with a balance of older and younger children in each group. Hand out Bibles and assign each group one of the following passages of Scripture: John 1:12; 1 Corinthians 2:9; Romans 8:17; and John 3:16.

Say: **Your job is to read your passage to discover what good things happen to people who put their faith in Jesus.** Give students about two minutes to read and discuss their passages. Then ask for a reporter from each group to share the group's discoveries. Possible responses may include

- John 1:12—they become children of God.
- 1 Corinthians 2:9—God prepares unimaginably wonderful things for them.
- Romans 8:17—they receive blessings from God with Christ.
- John 3:16—they'll live forever in heaven.

Say: **It's hard to imagine anyone saying "No, thanks" to God's love and all the wonderful things he offers us through Jesus. But sometimes it's hard to know just what to say to people and how to say it. Let's have some fun learning about a really different way to share your faith.**

LIFE APPLICATION

Dough-n't You Know God Loves You?

Have kids remain in four groups. Distribute scissors and the "Dough-n't You Know God Loves You?" handout (p. 86) to each student. Demonstrate how to fold and cut the handout to make an eight-page booklet. (See the illustrations in the margin.)

Say: **Your booklet contains a rap message about Jesus. Read through it aloud together in your group.** Give kids a few moments to read through the booklet. Then have each group choose a rapper to perform for the class. Assign page 3 of the booklet to one group, page 5 to another group, page 7 to a third group, and page 8 to the last group. Allow a couple of minutes for practice, then have the rappers from each group pop up and do the rap in sequence. Reward the rappers with a hearty round of applause.

Then say: **This is a great rap, not only because it's fun to do, but also because it tells about God's love and how people can receive forgiveness. ★ Jesus wants us to tell others about him. This rap is a fun way to do that. And here's something that can make sharing your faith even more fun.**

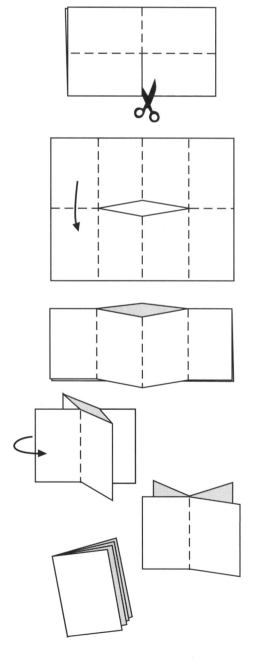

Before class, mix peanut butter and powdered sugar to make a soft, nonsticky dough. Give each student about one-third cup of dough in a plastic sandwich bag. Show kids how to model the dough into the shapes shown in the booklet—a person, a snake, a cross, and a crown.

Say: **You can make your own peanut butter dough at home by mixing peanut butter and powdered sugar. Then when you share the rap with your friends and use the dough to model the shapes in the booklet, you can leave your friends with a sweet reminder of God's love. Thinking back to the parable of the sower, this rap and this dough are seeds that you can plant to help God's kingdom grow! Now let's see what it might look like if God's kingdom started growing right here with the people in our class.**

Have kids set their dough and booklets aside.

COMMITMENT

God's Garden Grows!

Distribute scissors, colored pencils or markers, and photocopies of the "God's Garden" handout (p. 87). Demonstrate how to fold the handout in half then cut on the solid lines to make a repeating pattern. Have each student write his or her own name on the stem of the middle flower. On the petals of the flowers to the right and left, have kids write the names or initials of friends or relatives who don't know about Jesus—people with whom they can share God's love.

As kids are working, ask:

● **Besides using the booklet and rap, what are some other ways we can share God's love with people who don't know about Jesus?** (We can make friends with them; we can offer to pray for them when they're worried; we can be kind to them.)

Say: ★ **Jesus wants us to tell others about him, and there are lots of ways to do that. Using the rap is great, but sometimes we can show people Jesus' love just by being a friend or showing kindness. It's important to pray for people and ask God to help us show Jesus' love in the very best way. And that's how God's garden grows!**

Help kids hook each other's flower sections together by matching and sliding together the slits at the edges. Have kids tape or tack the "garden" to a wall. Cut off the right half-flower of your flower section and place your section at the left end of the display. As you work, say: **God's kingdom grows one person at a time. You never know when a seed of God's love may bloom in a person's heart, but when that happens, you've** helped another person become a child of God. And that's just about the best thing anyone on this earth can do!

CLOSING

Chain of Prayer

Say: ★ **Jesus wants us to tell others about him. Let's pray for each other and ask God to help us do that.**

Have kids stand in front of the flower sections they created. Begin a chain of prayer by praying for the person whose flower section is next to yours. Pray: **Lord, please help** (name of student) **share your love with** (person or people named on the flower). Then have that student pray the same prayer for the next person and so on. Have the last student come to the front of the line and pray for you and the person or people named on your flower. Close by having everyone say "amen" together.

Remind students to take their booklets and peanut butter dough with them.

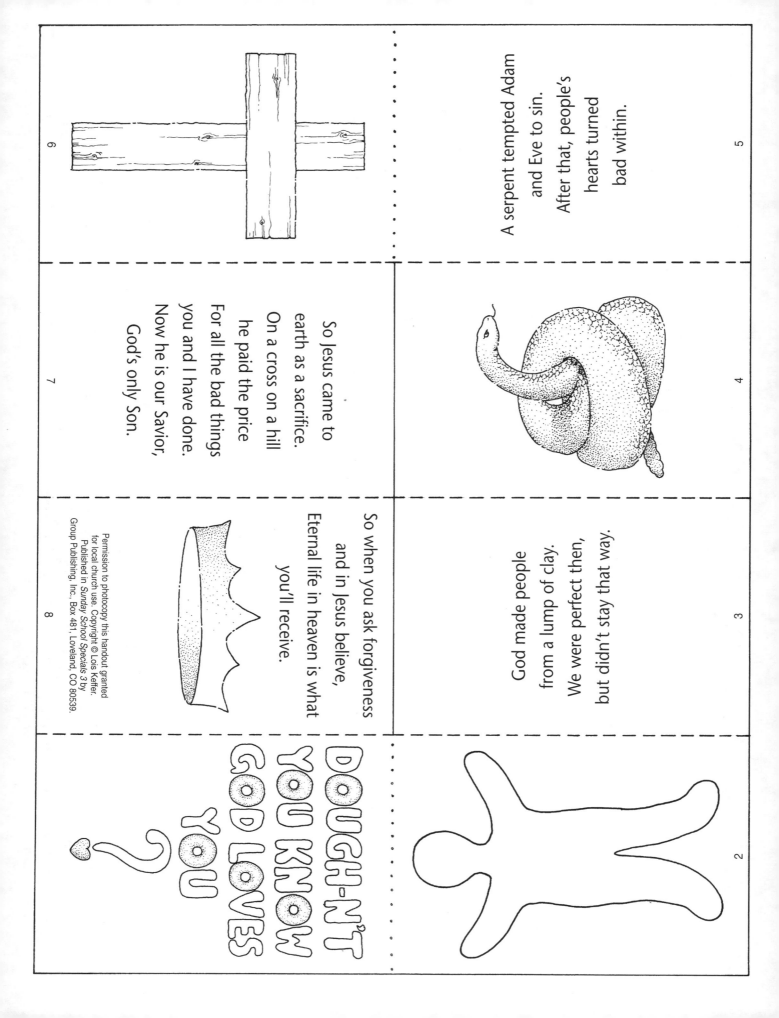

5

A serpent tempted Adam
and Eve to sin.
After that, people's
hearts turned
bad within.

6

4

7

So Jesus came to
earth as a sacrifice.
On a cross on a hill
he paid the price
For all the bad things
you and I have done.
Now he is our Savior,
God's only Son.

3

God made people
from a lump of clay.
We were perfect then,
but didn't stay that way.

8

So when you ask forgiveness
and in Jesus believe,
Eternal life in heaven is what
you'll receive.

2

DOUGH-N'T YOU KNOW GOD LOVES YOU?

GOD'S Garden

Fold on the center line, then cut on the solid lines. Unfold and cut the slits.

The Miraculous Catch

LESSON AIM

To help kids understand that ★ Jesus helps us when we're discouraged.

OBJECTIVES

Kids or families will
● brainstorm situations in which they feel discouraged,
● learn that the risen Jesus helped his discouraged disciples,
● discover that Jesus always has the power to help, and
● commit to trusting God in every situation.

YOU'LL NEED

❏ a rope
❏ fish-shaped crackers
❏ a Bible
❏ markers
❏ scissors
❏ transparent tape
❏ newsprint
❏ balloons
❏ photocopies of the "Sailing Through Discouragement" handout (p. 96)
❏ photocopies of the "Folded Fish-Basket" handout (p. 97)

NOTE

This lesson works well with an intergenerational class. You may wish to invite whole families to join you for this session.

John 21:1-14

In Jesus' third post-resurrection appearance to a group of his disciples, he appeared on the shore of the Sea of Galilee after several of the disciples had spent a long night fishing without success. The disciples saw a stranger on the shore who advised them to cast their nets on the right side of the boat. When the weary disciples accommodated the stranger, their net immediately bulged with a catch so large they couldn't haul it back into the boat. Taking a closer look at the helpful stranger, John said, "It is the Lord!" After struggling to bring their boat and miraculous catch of fish to shore, the disciples found that Jesus had made a fire and prepared a welcome breakfast of warm bread and grilled fish.

I'm always intrigued by the fact that the disciples made that one last toss of the net. Had I been in the boat, I probably would have sneered, "Yeah, right!" and rowed away. Jesus always helps us, but always in his time, in his way, and often after a great deal of effort on our part. Compare a night of fruitless fishing to a math concept that can't be conquered, an enemy who won't become a friend, or a hoped-for job that just doesn't materialize. Perseverance and faith are the qualities God nurtures in us as we hang on and keep trying, believing that God will make all things beautiful in his time.

Ephesians 4:29

Have you ever noticed how certain individuals generate a strong "personal atmosphere"? Some people radiate enthusiasm, good humor, sympathy, or a sense of calm. Others reflect pessimism, skepticism, or tension. This Scripture challenges us to be encouragers—positive people who consciously do and say what will build up others in the body of Christ.

UNDERSTANDING YOUR KIDS

How many times have you seen an art project that started with enthusiasm but ended up crumpled in a wastebasket? a hiker who couldn't wait to start up the trail but before long wanted to give up and turn back? a new school year marked by fresh determination that soured by the end of September? a long-saved-for purchase given up in favor of a lesser item that granted more immediate gratification? Ah, the frustrations of childhood!

Children lack the benefit of experience and the perspective it offers. That's why adults who are willing to offer help and encouragement are so crucial to kids' early successes. What a difference one compassionate, caring adult can make to a child who feels utterly hopeless when faced with taking a math test, making friends in a new place, or performing in a recital. As a teacher, that's just the kind of difference you're making in kids' lives each week. Congratulations and bless you! Children who've learned that they can count on help and encouragement from adults find it easy to put that same kind of trust in God. Use this lesson to help kids understand that Jesus is always there for them, and that unlike ordinary encouragers, he has unlimited power to help.

The Lesson ATTENTION GRABBER

Poor Kitty

As students arrive, have them help you place chairs in a circle. You'll need one less chair than there are people in class.

Say: **We're going to begin today with a really funny game called Poor Kitty. The person who's "It" has to kneel in front of someone who's sitting in a chair and meow. The person in the chair has to keep a perfectly straight face; pat It on the head; and say, "Poor Kitty." If the person in the chair cracks a smile or laughs, he or she is It. If the person doesn't smile, It goes to someone else and meows.**

Choose someone who's funny and outgoing to be It first. It may purr, make funny faces, meow several times, or rub his or her head on a player's knee. If you have time, play until everyone has had a chance to be It. Give a round of applause to the people who best resisted the impulse to smile, then ask:

● **In real life, what makes you laugh and smile?** (Jokes; when something good happens; when I see something funny on TV.)

● **When is it hard to make people smile?** (When bad things happen; when they're sick or tired.)

Say: **Turn to a partner and tell about a time you were really discouraged and didn't smile much at all.** Allow a couple of minutes for partners to share.

Then say: **Our Bible story today is about a bunch of really discouraged fishermen. Raise your hand if you've ever gone fishing and gotten discouraged.** Pause to let students briefly share their experiences. **The fishermen we're going to hear about just happened to be Jesus' disciples. They discovered in quite a unique way that ★ Jesus helps us when we're discouraged.**

What a Catch! (based on John 21:1-14)

Say: **To get ready for our story, we need a fishing boat, a big net, fishermen, and some fish.**

Using a length of rope, have students help you outline the shape of a boat in the middle of the floor. The outline should be large enough to hold several students. Recruit one-third of your students to be the "fishermen," Jesus' disciples. Have the fishermen stand near the boat. Have another third of your students be the "net." Instruct that group to join hands and sit on the floor near the boat. Have the remaining students be the "fish" and huddle on the opposite side of the boat from the net.

When everyone is in place, say: **We need to do one more thing before we begin the story. Fish and net groups, your part goes like this: "Ain't no fish, ain't no fish, ain't no fish here in this sea."** Have the fish and net groups use a rap beat and lots of enthusiasm as they repeat their line.

Fishermen, your part goes like this: "Baaad luck, baaad luck, sure seems like bad luck to me." Have the fishermen repeat their line. **Listen carefully and act out your part in the story. When I point to you, be ready to say your line. Here we go!**

One night, not long after Jesus rose from the dead, Peter said, "I'm going out to fish." Several other disciples said, "We'll go too." So they all hopped aboard their fishing boat. Cue the fishermen to get into the boat. **They pulled a big net into the boat, too, because they planned to catch a lot of fish.** Signal the fishermen to "pull" the net group into the boat.

At 11 o'clock, they threw their net into the water. Signal the net group to jump out of the boat. **But when they dragged the net back toward the boat, it was empty.**

Signal the net group to jump into the boat then shout along with the fish, "Ain't no fish, ain't no fish, ain't no fish here in this sea." Have the fishermen shake their heads and say, "Baaad luck, baaad luck, sure seems like bad luck to me."

At midnight, the fishermen threw their net into the water again. Signal the net group to jump out of the boat. **But when they dragged the net back toward the boat, it was empty.** Signal the net group to jump into the boat. Have the fish and net groups repeat their line, then have the fishermen repeat theirs.

Repeat this sequence for 1 o'clock, 2 o'clock, 3 o'clock, 4 o'clock, and 5 o'clock.

At 6 o'clock the fishermen were tired and discouraged. But then a stranger hailed them from the shore. "Friends," he called, "have you caught any fish?"

"No!" the discouraged fishermen called back.

"Throw your net on the other side of the boat!" the stranger shouted.

So the fishermen tossed the net on the other side of the boat. Have the net group scamper into the boat then jump out the other side. **Suddenly the net bulged with fish!** Have the fish group "swim" over and jump into the net.

Say: **Fish and net, say, "Check out the fish, check out the fish, check out the fish here in this sea!"** Pause for the fish and net groups to say their new line. **Fishermen, say, "Goood luck, goood luck, sure seems like good luck to me."** Pause for the fishermen to say their line.

The net was so full of fish that the fishermen couldn't even pull it back into the boat. Have the fishermen struggle to "pull" the net and fish then give up. **Then one of the fishermen pointed at the stranger on the shore. "That's no stranger," he said. "It's the Lord!"**

Sure enough, it was Jesus. And he had built a fire and had a hot, tasty breakfast ready for his tired, hungry disciples. And I have a tasty treat ready for you for doing such a good job with the Bible story.

Pour fish-shaped crackers into each student's cupped hands. Have the fishermen, net, and fish groups form separate circles and discuss these questions.

● **How do you think the disciples felt after fishing all night and catching nothing?** (Tired; discouraged; unhappy.)

● **If you had been in that boat, would you have wanted to toss the net out once more? Why or why not?** (Yes, because I don't like to give up; no, because I would have been sick of trying.)

● **Why do you think Jesus helped his disciples make this miraculous catch of fish?** (So they would still have faith in his power; because he loved them and didn't want them to be discouraged.)

Say: ★ **Jesus helps us when we're discouraged, just as he helped his disciples long ago. Let's find out what's discouraging to you and how Jesus can help us get through discouraging times.**

LIFE APPLICATION

Balloon Fish

Have students remain in their three groups. Give each group markers, scissors, transparent tape, and a sheet of newsprint. Give a balloon to each student. Have students blow up and tie off their balloons then draw fish faces on them.

Say: **Now set your balloon fish behind you for a moment. Choose a recorder for your group—someone who can write quickly. You'll also need a Bible reader and a reporter.** Pause for groups to choose people for those roles. **In just a moment I'll ask you to brainstorm with your group all the discouraging things you can think of—things such as getting the measles or getting cut from a team. At the end of two minutes, we'll share our lists of discouragements. Go!**

After two minutes, ask reporters to share their groups' lists.

Say: **Wow! That was terrible to listen to. I think we should stop and sob for a few seconds.** Lead the group in making loud sobbing sounds. **That's better. Now take your fish balloon and a marker. Write on your fish the three things you heard that would be the most discouraging to you. You may write things that have actually happened to you or things you hope never will happen to you. Some of you may need to help the younger kids write on their balloons. After you've all written on your balloons, tell your group what you wrote and why.**

Allow three or four minutes for sharing. Then say: **Enough of this doom and gloom! Now it's time to hear the good news straight from the Bible.**

Distribute photocopies of the "Sailing Through Discouragement" handout (p. 96). Have the readers in each group read aloud the three verses on the handout.

Then say: **These promises from the Bible can help us sail right through discouraging times. You'll notice that these verses are printed on fish tails and fins. I'd like you to cut them out and carefully tape them to your balloon fish. They'll help you remember that ★ Jesus helps us when we're discouraged.**

Demonstrate how to cut through the × in the fish tail and slip the tied end of the balloon through the cut. Students may want to curl the strips of the tail and fin pieces around a pencil. Then show kids how to use tape to attach the fins.

Say: **It's great to know that ★ Jesus helps us when we're discouraged. We can count on other people in God's family to encourage us too. Let's see how that works.**

Have students hold their balloons and form a circle. Say: **When I call out "fish," toss your balloons in the air if you were in that group. Then all of us will make sure those balloons stay in the air. We'll keep bopping them and try not to let any balloons fall to the ground. When I call out "nets," the members of that group will toss their balloons in the air. Finally I'll call out "fishermen," and the fishermen will toss their balloons in the air. Remember: We want to keep all the balloons in the**

TEACHER TIP

If you have adults in your class, encourage groups to list things that are discouraging to adults as well as to children.

TEACHER TIP

You may want to photocopy the "Sailing Through Discouragement" handout on neon yellow or orange paper. If you use white paper, encourage students to use colored pencils or markers to add colorful swirls or gradations of color to the fins and tails before they add them to the balloon fish.

air, so bee-bop-balloon-bop for all you're worth!

Call out "fish" then "nets" then "fishermen" at 15-second intervals. Keep the balloon bop going for about a minute and a half. Then call time and have students retrieve their own balloons, sit down, and take three deep breaths. Have a volunteer read Ephesians 4:29. Then ask:

● **What does this Bible verse tell us to do?** (Encourage each other; build each other up.)

● **Why is that important in God's family?** (Because we need each other; because God wants us to love each other as much as we love ourselves.)

● **How was what we did in this game like what this Bible verse tells us to do?** (We helped each other stay "up"; we tried to keep each other's balloons from falling.)

Say: **It's great to have brothers and sisters in Christ who we can count on to encourage us. It doesn't matter if you're older or younger or somewhere in the middle; a kind word of encouragement from you can really help someone get through a tough time. Let's have fun making an encouraging gift.**

COMMITMENT

A Basket of Encouragement

Before class make a sample fish basket from the "Folded Fish-Basket" handout (p. 97) to show the students.

Have students re-form their three groups. Distribute photocopies of the handout. Display your finished basket, then help students cut out and fold their own. You'll enjoy the "oohs" and "ahs" when students discover that pulling on the pointed ends of the folded pattern makes a basket suddenly appear!

Circulate among students as they work. Pour fish-shaped crackers into the baskets as students complete them. Ask:

● **How can a cheerful heart be like good medicine?** (A happy outlook makes me feel better; smiles help, no matter what goes wrong.)

● **When do you know that God is on your side?** (When I love and obey him; when I do what the Bible says.)

● **What does it mean to you that God is on your side?** (That I don't need to be afraid; that God will help me; that things will turn out for the best.)

● **How will the fish-shaped crackers in your basket remind you that ★ Jesus helps us when we're discouraged?** (I'll remember how he helped the disciples after their long night of fishing; I'll remember that Jesus can do anything and that he loves me just as he loved his disciples.)

94

Say: ★ **Jesus helps us when we're discouraged. Sometimes we find encouragement in God's Word, as with the verses printed on your baskets. Sometimes we find encouragement in prayer or in the way God makes things happen. And sometimes we find encouragement in each other.**

CLOSING

Baskets of Prayer

Have students gather in a circle with their completed baskets. Say: **Let's be silent for a moment. I'd like you to decide if you're going to keep your basket because you need encouragement or if you're going to give it away. Then I'll close with a prayer.**

Pause for a few moments, then pray: **Dear Jesus, thank you for the many ways you help us when we're discouraged. Help us to have cheerful hearts and to encourage each other, too. Amen.**

Remind students to take their baskets and balloon fish with them. You may want to set out extra "Folded Fish-Basket" handouts for students who want to make extra baskets to give away.

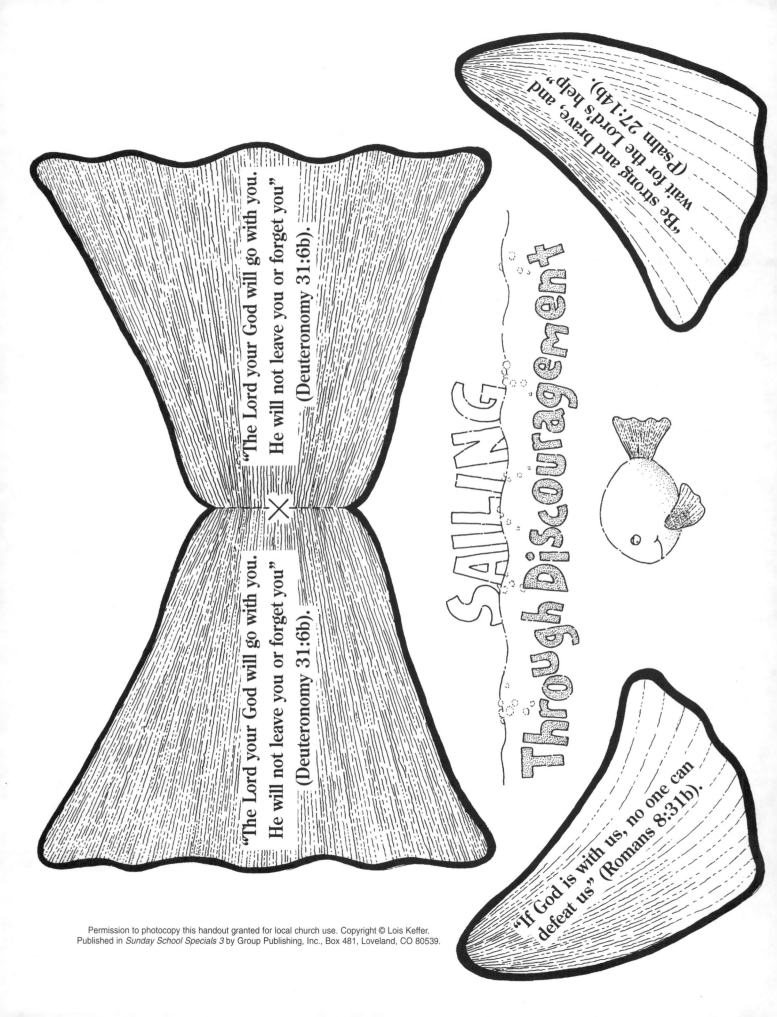

"The Lord your God will go with you. He will not leave you or forget you" (Deuteronomy 31:6b).

"The Lord your God will go with you. He will not leave you or forget you" (Deuteronomy 31:6b).

"Be strong and brave, and wait for the Lord's help" (Psalm 27:14b).

SAILING Through Discouragement

"If God is with us, no one can defeat us" (Romans 8:31b).

Folded Fish Basket

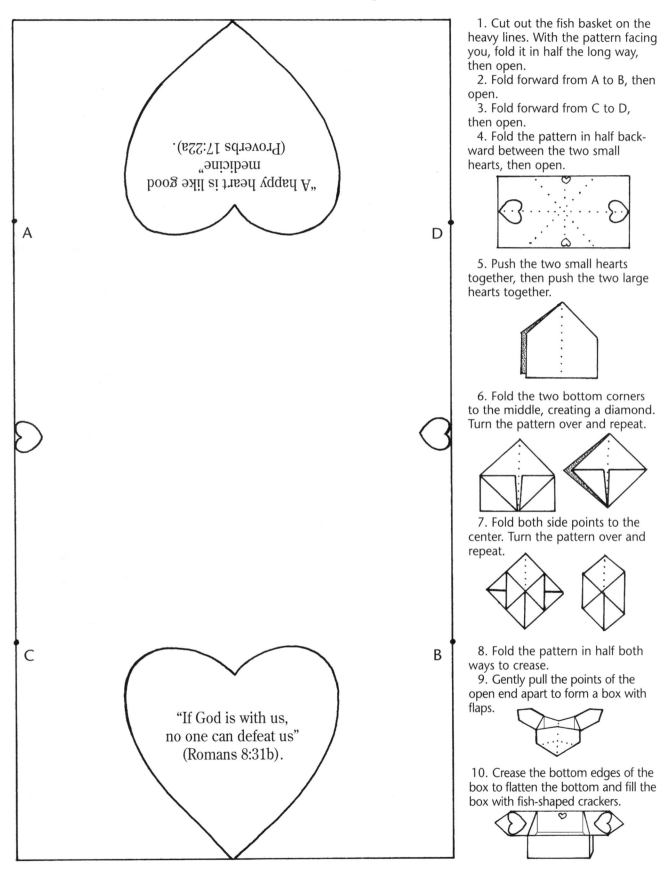

"A happy heart is like good medicine" (Proverbs 17:22a).

"If God is with us, no one can defeat us" (Romans 8:31b).

A

D

C

B

1. Cut out the fish basket on the heavy lines. With the pattern facing you, fold it in half the long way, then open.

2. Fold forward from A to B, then open.

3. Fold forward from C to D, then open.

4. Fold the pattern in half backward between the two small hearts, then open.

5. Push the two small hearts together, then push the two large hearts together.

6. Fold the two bottom corners to the middle, creating a diamond. Turn the pattern over and repeat.

7. Fold both side points to the center. Turn the pattern over and repeat.

8. Fold the pattern in half both ways to crease.

9. Gently pull the points of the open end apart to form a box with flaps.

10. Crease the bottom edges of the box to flatten the bottom and fill the box with fish-shaped crackers.

Prayer Power

LESSON AIM

To help kids understand that ★ God hears and answers our prayers.

OBJECTIVES

Kids or families will
- play a listening game,
- learn that God answered prayers for Peter's release,
- experience different ways to pray, and
- make a commitment to pray for each other.

NOTE

This lesson works well with an intergenerational class. You may wish to invite whole families to join you for this session.

YOU'LL NEED

❏ wrapped treats such as Hershey's Kisses or sugarless gum
❏ a photocopy of the "Peter's Escape" Bible story (pp. 102-103)
❏ Bibles
❏ modeling clay
❏ scissors
❏ markers
❏ photocopies of the "Praying Hands" handout (p. 107)

BIBLE BASIS

Acts 12:1-18

When King Herod had Peter arrested and thrown in prison, the situation looked grave indeed. Stephen's stoning had signaled the beginning of intense persecution in Jerusalem, causing Christians to flee and scatter across the Roman world. The Jerusalem Church was forced to meet covertly. Imagine the Church's horror when Herod arrested and executed the Apostle James, who was one of the two sons of Zebedee and one of Jesus' three closest companions. This brutality against Christians pleased the Jewish people, so Herod decided to boost his popularity by giving the same treatment to Peter. But God had other plans. In the dark of night, as earnest, frightened Christians prayed for God to deliver Peter from Herod's clutches, God sent an angel who freed Peter from his chains and led him past 16 sleeping guards and through the prison gate, which opened by itself. Peter himself could hardly believe what had happened—nor could the astonished prayer warriors who at first denied him entrance to the home where they were praying.

When I consider the greatness of our God, I have to smile and shake my head in wonder that we are nearly always surprised when God intervenes on our behalf. From our measly human perspective, the problems we face loom impossibly large; God seems quite distant, if not totally unreachable. Stories like Peter's deliverance from prison help correct our misapprehensions. God is GRRRRREAT! And he loves us. And he wants only the very best for us. Dare to pray boldly. Dare to believe that God, in his immeasurable power and love, can—and will—do unimaginably wonderful things to bring about his kingdom on earth.

Luke 11:1-4, 9-12

In these passages, Jesus depicts God as a caring Father who loves to do good things for his children. God is neither selfish, stingy, nor begrudging—he *wants* us to come to him with our needs. And he *wants* us to keep on asking, to be as persistent as a child. Society teaches us to be self-sufficient. God teaches us to be lovingly dependent.

UNDERSTANDING YOUR KIDS

No one has this business of prayer completely figured out, especially children. Most kids begin with rote prayers at meals and bedtime. Depending on denominational traditions, kids may or may not learn to pray extemporaneously until they're quite a bit older. They may be intimidated by prayers full of thees, thous, and other unfamiliar religious vocabulary. As teachers, it's important for us to model simple prayers, not only so that kids can understand them, but also because speaking to God in everyday language makes God seem more real, more present, and more accessible. There's nothing more heartwarming than a child's unaffected prayer. This is what we should encourage.

We want kids to learn that God is always happy to listen to them and that God wants our prayers to be a natural part of our daily lives. Use this lesson to teach kids that there are many different ways to experience meaningful prayer.

The Lesson

ATTENTION GRABBER

All Ears

As students arrive, have them help you arrange chairs in a circle. If space is limited, make the circle two rows deep.

Say: **We're going to start off today with a really fun game called All Ears. I'm going to ask several questions. As soon as you think you know the answer, pop up. If you pop up before I finish the question, you'll have to finish the question correctly before you can give me an answer. If the first person to pop up answers incorrectly, the second person will get a chance, and so on. The first person to answer the question correctly will get a treat.** Hold up a bag of treats. **If no one answers correctly, I get to keep all the treats! Ready to pop up? Here we go.**

Read the following questions clearly and at a deliberate pace.

● **What is the 10th letter of the alphabet?** (J)

● **How many dwarfs became friends of Snow White?** (Seven)

● **When is Valentine's Day?** (February 14)

● **Who was the first president of the United States?** (George Washington)

● **How many letters are in the word "scribble"?** (Eight)

● **What's the opposite of upside down?** (Right side up)

● **How many bears lived in the house Goldilocks visited?** (Three)

● **What was President Kennedy's middle name?** (Fitzgerald)

● **Whose red slippers helped her return from Oz?** (Dorothy's)

● **What's the sixth word of the "Star-Spangled Banner"?** (By)

Say: **I think everyone will know the answer to this last question so I'd like you all to pop up and say it together.**

● **Who loves you so much that he died for you and wants you to live in heaven with him forever?** (Jesus!)

Toss treats to all parts of the room so everyone has at least one.

Then say: **Let's set up a scale of 1 to 10. One means that you weren't listening at all. Ten means that you were all ears.**

● **How would you rate how well you were listening?** Let several students reply. Most will name numbers near the top of the scale.

● **What made you listen so well?** (I wanted to be first; I wanted to win a treat.)

● **How well do you listen when Mom says to clean your room?** (I'd give myself a 2 or 3.)

● **How well do you listen when you're starving and someone calls out, "Dinner is ready"?** (A 9 or 10.)

Say: **Sometimes we listen well, and sometimes we don't. It usually depends on whether we think we'll hear something we want to hear. But there's someone who always listens well. Someone who never misses a word we say. Someone who listens just because he loves us.**

● **Who do you think that person is?** (God; Jesus.)

Say: **Today we're going to learn that ★ God hears and answers our prayers. Not because he gets a treat. Not because we're going to do him a big favor. Not because we're good at praying and we always go to church. Nope— God *loves* us, and that's why he hears and answers our prayers. Many times, God answers our prayers in ways we hadn't dreamed of. That's exactly what happens in the Bible story we're going to hear today.**

BIBLE STUDY

Peter's Escape (Acts 12:1-18)

Photocopy the story "Peter's Escape" (pp. 102-103) and cut apart the verses. Have students form pairs or trios, then have the groups all sit together in one large circle. Distribute the 20 verses of the Bible story among the pairs or trios as evenly as possible. Make sure you keep the verses in order as you distribute them around the circle.

Have students decide which person in each pair or trio will read the verse as the other one or two people lead the actions. Encourage students to read their sections with a lively rap beat.

Allow a couple of minutes for students to prepare their sections, then give the cue to begin the story.

It's a good idea to go through the story twice to let students polish their performances a bit and to make sure they understand the plot of this exciting story. After the second time through, collect the verses and have students give themselves a round of applause.

Peter's Escape

(based on Acts 12:1-18)

1

Mean King Herod was on Peter's tail *(make a mean face, hands on hips)*
And had him locked up tight in jail. *(Cross arms over chest.)*

2

Sixteen soldiers—that's eight plus eight *(flash eight fingers twice)*—
Stood guard in the cell and around the gate. *(Stand at attention.)*

3

One, two, three, four, five, six, seven. *(Hold up fingers as you count.)*
Peter's friends prayed to God in heaven. *(Fold hands and look up.)*

4

Seven, six, five, four, three, and two. *(Count backward on fingers.)*
I see an angel here *(clap)*—don't you? *(Shield eyes, then clap.)*

5

The angel woke Peter and said, "Time to hurry. *(Pretend to shake someone.)*
I'll help you escape King Herod's fury." *(Make a beckoning motion.)*

6

Peter's chains fell off with a clink, clank, DWING! *(Look at open hands.)*
Said the angel, "Get dressed— that's the next thing." *(Hold up a make-believe shirt.)*

7

So Peter got dressed in his coat and shoes *(pretend to put on shoes)*
While those big, scary guards just took a little snooze. *(Tilt head to the side and snore.)*

8

Peter followed the angel right out of the cell *(walk in place)*
And thought, "Is this a dream? I really can't tell." *(Point to head, then shrug.)*

9

Then the gate swung open with a big old CREAK *(swing arm like a gate opening)*,
And none of the guards even took a peek. *(Snore.)*

10

Peter and the angel walked straight ahead *(walk in place)*
While most of the town was asleep in bed. *(Rest cheek on folded hands.)*

11

They walked in the light of the
moon that shone (walk in place),
Then suddenly Peter was all alone.
(Look around, surprised.)

12

He scratched his head, and he
looked around (scratch head)
And said, "Here I am in the middle
of town." (Put hands on hips
and look around.)

13

"An amazing thing just happened
to me. (Put hands to cheeks.)
The Lord sent an angel to set me
free!" (Spread open arms.)

14

Peter knew that all his friends were
praying (fold hands),
So he went right over to where they
were staying. (Walk in place.)

15

He pounded on the door with a
knock, knock, knock (pretend
to knock),
And when Rhoda answered, she
had quite a shock. (Gasp.)

16

For she knew very well it was
Peter's voice (put hand to ear),
So she ran and told the others,
"It's Peter—rejoice!" (Run in
place and point.)

17

Peter waited outside impatiently
(cross arms and tap foot)
'Til the others came running to
the door to see. (Run in place.)

18

They pushed the front door open
wide (pretend to open a door),
And there was Peter, standing
outside. (Smile and wave.)

19

"Shh!" Peter said. "Let me tell my
tale. (Bring finger to lips.)
An angel just set me free from jail."
(Pretend to pull doors open.)

20

That's what happens when people pray. (Fold hands.)
So pray for the people you love
each day! (Cross hands over
heart.)

Ask:

● **Why were Peter's friends surprised when he came to the door?** (It seemed impossible for him to escape from prison; they never thought about God sending an angel to set Peter free.)

● **Who can tell about a time an answer to prayer really surprised you?** Let several students share their experiences. You may want to "prime the pump" by sharing an answer to prayer you've received.

After students have shared, say: **As you can see, ★ God hears and answers our prayers today just as he did long ago. Let's look at what Jesus said about prayer, then let's discover some special ways we can pray.**

LIFE APPLICATION

Ways to Pray

Have students remain in the pairs or trios they formed for the Bible story. Give each group a Bible.

Say: **The Bible tells us that Jesus often went away by himself to pray. Once when he returned from praying, the disciples asked him to teach them something. You can discover their request and Jesus' answer in Luke 11:1-4. Choose a reader to read that passage aloud for your group.**

Give groups a couple of minutes to find and read Luke 11:1-4. Then ask:

● **Why do you think the disciples asked Jesus to teach them to pray?** (Because they saw that prayer was important to Jesus; because Jesus prayed a lot; because there's a lot to learn about prayer.)

● **What part of Jesus' prayer gives praise to God?** (The first two lines; the first part.)

● **Why is it important to praise God when we pray?** (It reminds us of all God has done for us; it helps us think about God instead of just thinking about what we want.)

● **What things did Jesus ask for?** (Food; forgiveness of sins; help in avoiding temptation.)

Say: **Jesus encouraged his followers to ask God for what they needed. Look a little further to verses 9 through 12.**

Have a volunteer read that passage to the class. Then ask:

● **Why does God give us good things?** (Because he loves us like a father; because he's powerful and he loves us.)

Say: **★ God hears and answers our prayers because he loves us and he loves to do good things for us. There are many, many ways to pray. Jesus gave this prayer as an example. Let's experience this prayer a different way right now. In** just a moment I'll ask you to close your eyes. As I read the Lord's Prayer aloud, I'd like you to make up motions for it. Don't worry about how you look or what you do, because everyone's eyes will be closed. Just make up actions that show what the prayer means. Ready? Close your eyes.

Read Luke 11:2-4 aloud as students act out the prayer.

Then say: **That's just one way you can experience prayer. Now let's explore some other exciting ways to pray.**

● **Walking Prayer**—Take a silent walk around the halls of your church. Pause outside each classroom to pray for the people inside. Gather around the pulpit where the pastor or priest will speak and pray for that day's message. At each location you may want to pray silently or ask a volunteer to briefly pray aloud.

● **One-Word Prayers**—Gather everyone in a circle and hold hands. Explain that you're going to pray one-word prayers. The one word might express a feeling, a concern, or a thanks, or it might be the name of a person. Encourage students to pray as many times as they wish but to make each prayer only one word. The discipline of using only one word helps students focus on what's most important to communicate to God.

● **Potters' Prayers**—Have students form pairs or trios. Give each student a small amount of modeling clay or dough. You may wish to play quiet praise songs as each student forms an object that represents an important prayer concern. Encourage students to pray as they form the clay. When most people have finished modeling their objects, give a 30-second warning, then call time. Invite volunteers to share their prayer concerns with their group members and to show what they modeled. Make sure no one feels pressured to share.

After your prayer experiences, have everyone re-form their pairs or trios to discuss the following questions:

● **What did these experiences teach you about prayer that you didn't know before?** (That there are different ways to pray; that I can pray creatively.)

● **How will what we did today affect the way you pray in the future?** (I'll try different kinds of prayers; I'll be open to new ways of praying.)

● **Who wants to share another unique way of praying you've experienced?**

Allow two or three minutes for discussion, then call everyone together and invite volunteers to share what they discussed in their groups.

Say: ★ **God hears and answers our prayers, no matter how or where we pray. Now let's make reminders of the kinds of prayers we've experienced today.**

TEACHER TIP

You'll find suggestions on this page for three other creative prayer experiences. Use any or all of them, depending on their compatibility with your church's traditions and on the amount of remaining class time.

COMMITMENT

Praying-Hands Autographs

Distribute scissors, markers, and photocopies of the "Praying Hands" handout (p. 107). Ask a volunteer to read the verse at the bottom of the handout aloud. Ask other students to rephrase the verse in their own words. Have students fold the paper in half and cut out the praying hands then open the paper and leave it flat.

Then say: **I hope you've learned today that God enjoys hearing from us! God encourages us again and again in his Word to come to him with our needs, with our praise, and with our concerns for others. ★ God hears and answers our prayers! You'll see that this handout reminds you of different ways you can pray. But I also want it to be a reminder to pray for each other.**

On the blank side of your handout, write your name and draw a heart around it. The heart is to remind you that God loves you. Then we'll start trading our handouts and signing our names on each other's. The names will serve two purposes: They'll remind you to pray for those people, and they'll remind you that all those people are praying for you!

Allow time for students to sign each other's handout. Then gather everyone in a circle. Show students how to fold back the tabs on their handouts and hook the slits together so the praying hands stand up. Have students place their praying hands on the floor in front of them.

CLOSING

Prayers All Around

Pray: **Dear Lord, thank you for loving us enough to hear and answer our prayers. Help us get into the good habit of talking to you several times a day. And help us support each other in our prayers. In Jesus' name, amen.**

As you close, have each student shake hands with every other student and say, "I'll be praying for you."

PRAYING HANDS

Fold this paper in half on the dotted line, then cut out the praying hands on the heavy, solid line. Carefully fold back the tabs on each side at the bottom and cut the slits. Hook the slits together to make your praying hands stand up.

Walking Prayer

Take a walk anywhere. As you walk, pray silently for the people you pass and the people who live in the houses or stores you pass.

Potters' Prayers

Make a clay model to represent something you're concerned about. Pray as you model the clay. Let the clay model remind you to trust God.

Personalize the Lord's Prayer

Read the Lord's Prayer from Matthew 6:9-13. As you read, substitute the word "I" for "we," "me" for "us," and "my" for "our."

One-Word Prayers

Before a meal, take turns saying one-word prayers. The word might be "thanks" or "help" or the name of a person you're concerned about. Each person may want to say several one-word prayers.

"Do not worry about anything, but pray and ask God for everything you need, always giving thanks" (Philippians 4:6).

When the Heat Is On

(a lesson for back to school or any time)

LESSON AIM

To help kids understand that ★ God helps us stand up for what's right.

OBJECTIVES

Kids will
- play a mismatched game;
- learn how God helped Shadrach, Meshach, and Abednego when they stood up for what was right;
- develop responses to situations involving peer pressure; and
- affirm each other's commitment to doing what's right.

YOU'LL NEED

- ❏ masking tape
- ❏ table tennis balls
- ❏ a whistle
- ❏ a photocopy of the "Statue and the Fourth Man" figures (p. 118)
- ❏ photocopies of the "Three Men and the Flames" figures (p. 119)
- ❏ gold paper or shiny gold gift wrap
- ❏ scissors
- ❏ beige paper
- ❏ red paper
- ❏ a Bible
- ❏ a photocopy of the "Hot Spots" cards (p. 120)

Daniel 3:1-30

When our kids were little, we would say, "Hot! Hot! Hot!" to warn them away from objects that might burn them. King Nebuchadnezzar made it very clear to Shadrach, Meshach, and Abednego just how "Hot! Hot! Hot!" things would get if they didn't bow before his massive golden statue. But in the face of royal wrath, the three Hebrew heroes kept their cool. "The God we serve is able to save us from the furnace" seemed clear enough to inform the king of their intention to disobey. But then they added, "But even if God does not save us, we want you, O king, to know this: We will not serve your gods or worship the gold statue you have set up." Wowie zowie! No careful diplomacy here. These guys were ready and willing to take the heat.

Where did this holy audacity come from? Absolute faith in the fact that "the Lord our God, the Lord is one" and that the gold statue standing on the plain was nothing more than a pathetic imitation—a gaudy symbol of a king's pride. So when the king pulled a power play, the three valiant Hebrews stood their ground. Their courage and God's miraculous deliverance changed a king's heart and taught a pagan empire to humble itself before the true God. Today, as in ancient times, courage is born of absolute confidence in the power of God and the truth of his Word. Because we can't see God with human eyes, we sometimes let ourselves be intimidated by the flames. But God hasn't changed. When we stand up for what's right, there's a great, big, omnipotent God right behind us, in front of us, and all around us.

Matthew 7:13-14

Jesus tells us that a broad road leads to destruction and that a narrow road leads to life. This statement helps us understand why we Christians seem to be swimming upstream most of our lives, struggling against a culture that proclaims our beliefs unenlightened and narrow-minded. Let's prepare our kids to swim against the current!

UNDERSTANDING YOUR KIDS

As you approach this lesson on peer pressure, it's important to be familiar with the varying backgrounds of the kids in your class. Some may be home-schooled and largely sheltered from peer pressure. Some may attend Christian schools where pressure to get involved in negative behaviors may be somewhat less than in public schools but is by no means nonexistent. Kids who attend public schools may feel like veterans of peer-pressure battles even in the early grades. If your class is diverse, encourage kids to use this opportunity to learn what school life is like for others, without claiming that any one learning environment is superior to another. This can be a divisive issue among Christians. The safest position to take is one of mutual understanding and respect.

The overriding fact is that all kids will face peer pressure someday, and it's never too soon to prepare. Use this lesson to help kids see that God will be with them when they stand up for what's right and that they never need to be embarrassed to take a stand for Christ.

The Lesson   ATTENTION GRABBER

Blown Away

Before class divide an open area of your classroom in half by placing a line of masking tape on the floor. Then put down two more lines, one foot to each side of the first. Set four table tennis balls on the middle line.

As kids arrive, have them count off by fours. Have the ones, twos, and threes line up on one side of the room. Have the fours line up on the other side.

Say: **Let's play a game to discover who the real windbags in our class are. I've placed four table tennis balls on the center line. The lines on either side of the center are the safety lines. Your job is to try to blow the balls across the other team's safety line. No part of your head or body may cross your safety line. You may blow from any position—sitting, squatting, or lying on your stomach. When a ball gets past your safety line, the other team gets a point. When I blow the whistle, we'll place all the balls on the center line and start another round. Ready, set, blow!**

If the fours protest that their team is much smaller than the other, tell them not to worry and that everything will turn out right.

Blow the whistle as soon as all the table tennis balls are blown past the safety lines. Then reset the balls and begin another round. Ignore the protests of the fours and continue play for three or four rounds. Then collect the balls and gather everyone in a circle. Ask:

● **Were you surprised at how lopsided the score turned out to be? Explain.** (No, because one team had so many more players; yes, because the smaller team scored even though it didn't

110

have as many players.)

Ask the ones, twos, and threes:

● **What was it like being on the larger team?** (Cool, because we got the most points; fun, because we didn't have to work as hard; not so fun, because I felt sorry for the people on the other team.)

Ask the fours:

● **What was it like being on your team?** (Discouraging, because we were so outnumbered; fun, because we worked well together.)

● **If we played this again, which team would you choose to be on? Explain.** (The bigger one, because it would win; the smaller one, because it's more of a challenge.)

● **How was being on the smaller team like being a Christian in your school or neighborhood?** (We're outnumbered; it feels as if there are a lot of people against us; it's not, because I go to a Christian school.)

● **Who can tell about a time you felt really outnumbered because you're a Christian?** Allow two or three students to share.

Say: **Today we're going to learn that ★ God helps us stand up for what's right. That's pretty easy when we're surrounded by a lot of Christian friends. Then we're on the bigger team. But it can be hard when there are only a few Christians. Then we might feel outnumbered and blown away, just as the smaller team in our game did. But whether we're many or few, ★ God helps us stand up for what's right.**

Our Bible story today is about three young men who stood up for what was right when they were completely outnumbered—and it could have cost them their lives.

BIBLE STUDY

The Fiery Furnace (based on Daniel 3:1-30)

Before class photocopy the "Statue and the Fourth Man" figures (p. 118) onto gold paper or trace them on shiny gold gift wrap. Cut the two figures apart on line 1.

Copy the "Three Men and the Flames" figure (p. 119) onto beige paper. Lay a sheet of red paper under the beige paper. When you cut out the three men, only the beige paper will show. When you cut out and fold up the fire, the flames will be red.

Set the scissors and the photocopied figures beside you. Say: **Long ago in the land of Babylon, there lived a great king named Nebuchadnezzar. King Nebuchadnezzar decided to make a huge statue.**

Fold the statue figure in half on line 2. (See diagram 1.)

TEACHER TIP

Practice cutting and folding the figures before class so you can do it confidently as you tell the story.

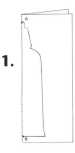
1.

111

2.

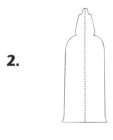

3.

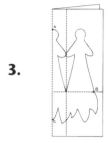

4.

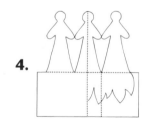

We're talkin' really huge—as tall as 15 tall basketball players standing on top of each other's shoulders! The king had this giant statue covered with pure gold.

Cut the statue figure from A to B.

Imagine how it gleamed in the sun.

Unfold the statue figure (diagram 2).

The king was proud of his statue—so proud, in fact, that he wanted everyone to bow down and worship it. So the king made a rule. Every time the horns, pipes, flutes, and other instruments played, anyone who didn't bow down and worship the statue would be thrown into a fiery furnace.

That was a problem for three men named Shadrach, Meshach, and Abednego.

Fold the beige paper in half on line 1 (diagram 3).

Cut the men from A to B, then cut to the right edge of the paper to remove the top section.

They were Jews who'd been forced to lived in Babylon after the Babylonian army defeated the army of Judah. Even though they lived in exile, Shadrach, Meshach, and Abednego still worshiped God and obeyed God's Word. God's Word teaches that we should worship only the one, true God. So Shadrach, Meshach, and Abednego weren't about to bow down to the king's gold statue—even if it meant being thrown in a fiery furnace.

Fold the three men again, this time on line 2.

Cut out and remove section 3.

But everyone else in Babylon did exactly what the king had ordered. When the horns, pipes, flutes, and other instruments played, they bowed down. But Shadrach, Meshach, and Abednego stood straight up.

Unfold the figure of the three men and hold it up (diagram 4).

As you can imagine, there were nasty people who just couldn't wait to tell King Nebuchadnezzar about the three Jews who stood straight up when everyone else bowed down. When the king heard about them, he was furious.

"Bring those men to me!" he shouted. So Shadrach, Meshach, and Abednego came before the king.

"Is it true that you do not serve my gods or bow down to my golden statue?" he demanded. "I'll give you one more chance. If you bow down the next time the instruments play, everything will be OK. But if you refuse to bow down, you'll be thrown immediately into a blazing furnace. Then what god will rescue you?"

Shadrach, Meshach, and Abednego replied, "If you throw us into the furnace, our God can rescue us. But even if he doesn't, we will not serve your gods or worship your golden statue."

The king flew into a rage. "Heat the furnace seven times hotter than usual!" he ordered. "You soldiers over there—tie these men up and throw them in the fire!"

Fold the three men in half on the middle line (diagram 5).
Cut from B to C.

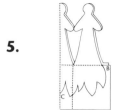

5.

So the soldiers tied up Shadrach, Meshach, and Abednego and pushed them into the furnace. The roaring flames leaped out of the furnace and killed the soldiers.

Unfold the three men and fold up the flames on line 4 so they are in front of the three men (diagram 6).

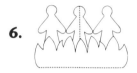

6.

But Shadrach, Meshach, and Abednego weren't hurt at all. In fact, they were walking around inside the furnace.

King Nebuchadnezzar jumped up and stared into the fire, amazed.

Fold the figure of the fourth man in half on line 3 (diagram 7).
Cut the fourth man from C to D.

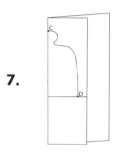

7.

"Didn't we throw three men into the fire?" he asked.

Cut off the fourth man figure on line 4, then hold the fourth man behind the three men in the fire (diagram 8).

8.

"I see four men walking around in there. They're not tied up, and they're not hurt at all! The fourth man looks like a son of the gods!"

Then the king walked right up to the furnace and called out, "Shadrach, Meshach, and Abednego, servants of the Most High God, come out! Come here!"

Shadrach, Meshach, and Abednego came out of the fire. Everyone crowded around in amazement. Their clothes weren't burned; their hair wasn't singed—they didn't even smell of smoke!

Let's read the end of this story straight from the Bible.

Have a good dramatic reader look up and read aloud Daniel 3:28-30.

Then say: **Let's have a round of applause for our three brave men! Now close your eyes for a moment. Think of a furious, raging king standing right in front of you.** Pause for a moment. **Think of a roaring, ravenous fire right behind you.** Pause again. **Now open your eyes.** Ask:

● **If you'd been in Shadrach, Meshach, and Abednego's place, what do you think you'd have done?** Allow several students to respond.

● **Do you think they did the right thing? Explain.** (Yes, because they knew it was more important to obey God than to obey the king; yes, because God expects us to obey his Word no matter what.)

● **What made Shadrach, Meshach, and Abednego so brave?** (They trusted God's power; they believed God was more powerful than the king.)

● **Why do you think God sent a heavenly guardian to protect Shadrach, Meshach, and Abednego?** (Because it would show the king and his officials that only God is the true God; because God loved the three men.)

● **What good things happened as a result of the three men standing up for what was right?** (A king believed in God; the whole empire was ordered not to say anything against God.)

Say: **Shadrach, Meshach, and Abednego's brave stand made a huge difference. The proud king learned to honor God and commanded that everyone else in his kingdom respect God. The three men were promoted to more important positions in the government, where they could tell even more people about God. Standing up for what's right isn't always easy, but it can make a huge difference. It may change one person's heart or even a whole kingdom. That's why ★ God helps us stand up for what's right.**

LIFE APPLICATION

Hot Spots

Before class photocopy and cut apart the "Hot Spots" cards (p. 120). Say: **Not too many people are thrown in fiery furnaces today. But that doesn't mean you don't run into hot spots. I'll show you what I mean.**

Pick up the table tennis balls from the opening activity. As you toss them in the air, say: **Catch these—quick!** Give a "Hot Spots" card to each student who caught a ball.

Say: **Quickly form a group with the card-holder nearest you. Read the card aloud together and brainstorm what you would do in the situation described on the card. I'll give you one minute to prepare, then each card-holder will report to the class. Go!**

Blow your whistle after one minute. Then have card-holders read their cards and tell their groups' responses. After each response, allow the rest of the class to suggest other possible responses. Then collect the used cards and have students form a cluster in front of you.

Say: **This time when I toss the table tennis balls, stand still with your arms at your sides. The people the balls touch first will be the card-holders for this round.** Toss the balls gently in the air, then give the remainder of the "Hot Spots" cards to the students touched first by each ball.

Say: **Quickly form groups around the card-holders, just like last time. You'll have one minute to read your cards and come up with responses. Go!**

Call time after one minute and have groups read their cards and give responses. Allow the rest of the students to suggest other possible responses to each situation. Then collect the cards and ask:

● **How was getting the cards like the way you get caught in hot spots in real life?** (Sometimes it's surprising; you never know when it's going to happen; you may try to avoid it, but you can't.)

● **Why do Christians often end up in hot spots like these?** (Because we live by God's rules; because we try to obey God and other people don't.)

Say: **Jesus had something interesting to say about going against the crowd.** Have a volunteer read Matthew 7:13-14 aloud. Then ask:

● **What do you think Jesus meant when he said that the way that leads to life is narrow?** (He meant that God set a certain path for us to follow; that God's way is different from the way most people go.)

● **Why is it that few people choose to go God's way?** (Because they don't want to obey God; because they want to do things their own way.)

● **How does Jesus' statement help explain why Christians have to battle peer pressure?** (It tells us to expect only a few people to take the narrow way; it tells us that most people will miss the way to life.)

Say: **Jesus told his followers to expect to go against the crowd. But he also said something to encourage us.** Have volunteers read John 14:15-17 and 16:33. Ask:

● **How did Jesus overcome the world?** (He rose from the dead; he took our sins for us.)

Say: **Before Jesus went back to heaven, he promised to send a helper—the Holy Spirit. When we find ourselves in hot spots, we can say a quick prayer and ask the Holy Spirit to help us. That's one way ★ God helps us stand up for what's right. Let's discover another way we can find courage and help to stand up for what's right.**

COMMITMENT

Rap It Up

Say: **As I read this Scripture passage, listen carefully for four things the writer, Paul, tells Christians to do. Each time you hear one of those four things, wave your hand in the air, then put it down. Here we go.**

"Only one thing concerns me: Be sure that you live in a way that brings honor to the Good News of Christ.

Then . . . I will hear that you are standing strong with one purpose, that you work together as one for the faith of the Good News, and that you are not afraid of those who are against you" (Philippians 1:27-28a).

● **What does Paul tell Christians to do?** (Live in a way that brings honor to Christ; stand strong with one purpose; work together as one; don't be afraid of those who are against you.)

Say: **When we do all those things, we help each other stand up for what's right. That's called positive peer pressure. Shadrach, Meshach, and Abednego supported each other in their stand against the king. That positive peer pressure helped them do what was right even though it could have cost them their lives. We can influence each other with positive peer pressure too.** Ask:

● **Who can tell about a time when having other Christians around helped you do what was right?** Allow two or three students to share.

Say: **Let's make a reminder of the brave stand Shadrach, Meshach, and Abednego took and of how they helped each other.**

Distribute scissors and photocopies of the "Three Men and the Flames" figures (p. 119). Lead students step-by-step through the folding and cutting sequence from the Bible story. When everyone has cut out a figure, have kids form a circle, then lead them in reading aloud the rap that's printed on the flames. If you have young nonreaders in your class, go over the words twice and have them repeat each line after you. Then teach kids the motions printed below.

When peer pressure's pushin' *(push forward three times)*,
And it's feelin' kinda tight *(crunch arms close to your sides and rock from side to side)*,
Just remember that it's cool *(shake a finger, then give someone a high five on "cool")*
To stand up for what's right! *(Wave arms high, then let arms rest on the shoulders of people beside you.)*

For extra fun after kids have learned the rap and motions, have them form two lines facing each other. Have one group say the first line, then have the other group say the second line. On the third line, have kids give high fives to people they're facing in the opposite group. On the fourth line, have them step together and rest their arms on each other. (Each student will be facing the opposite direction of the person on either side of him or her.)

Let students practice the rap several times. Then gather everyone in a circle and say: ★ **God helps us stand up for what's right. One way God helps us is by giving us Christian friends.**

Right now I'd like you to give a handshake or a high five to all the other students and say, "I'm gonna' help you do what's right." Let's see how quickly we can all shake hands and say that to each other.

CLOSING

Pile-of-Hands Prayer

After handshakes and high fives, gather students in a huddle and have them make a pile of hands in the center. Close with a prayer similar to this one: **Dear Lord, please give us courage to stand up for what's right even when it's hard or scary. Help us to encourage each other. In Jesus' name, amen.**

Line 3

C

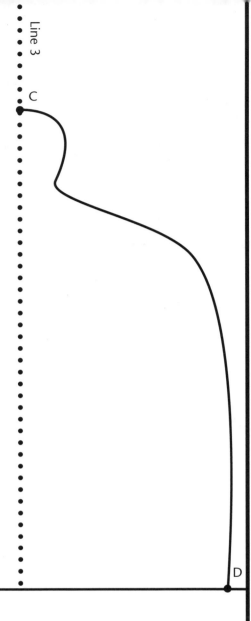

D

Line 4

Line 1

The Statue and the Fourth Man

A

B

Line 2

The Three Men and the Flames

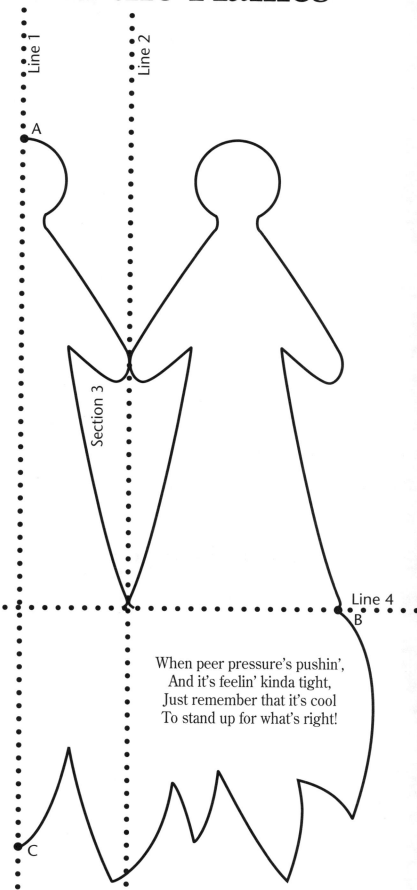

Line 1

Line 2

A

Section 3

Line 4

B

C

When peer pressure's pushin',
And it's feelin' kinda tight,
Just remember that it's cool
To stand up for what's right!

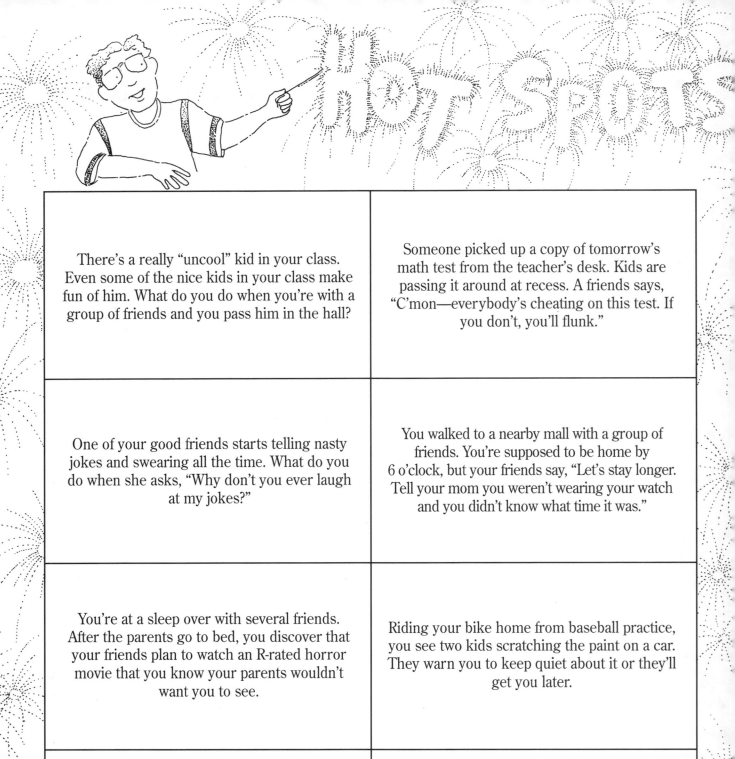

There's a really "uncool" kid in your class. Even some of the nice kids in your class make fun of him. What do you do when you're with a group of friends and you pass him in the hall?

Someone picked up a copy of tomorrow's math test from the teacher's desk. Kids are passing it around at recess. A friends says, "C'mon—everybody's cheating on this test. If you don't, you'll flunk."

One of your good friends starts telling nasty jokes and swearing all the time. What do you do when she asks, "Why don't you ever laugh at my jokes?"

You walked to a nearby mall with a group of friends. You're supposed to be home by 6 o'clock, but your friends say, "Let's stay longer. Tell your mom you weren't wearing your watch and you didn't know what time it was."

You're at a sleep over with several friends. After the parents go to bed, you discover that your friends plan to watch an R-rated horror movie that you know your parents wouldn't want you to see.

Riding your bike home from baseball practice, you see two kids scratching the paint on a car. They warn you to keep quiet about it or they'll get you later.

You're building models in your friend's garage. He holds up a spray can and says, "I've heard that just a few whiffs of this stuff make you feel really cool. Let's try it. It can't be that bad if they sell it in the store."

It's the day before summer vacation. Several of your friends plan to cut class after lunch. They say, "You've gotta cut class too, or you'll ruin it for everybody. C'mon—don't be a nerd."

Thanks-Living

11

(a lesson for Thanksgiving or any time)

LESSON AIM

To help kids understand that ★ all good things come from God.

OBJECTIVES

Kids will
- pop balloons and receive prizes,
- give thanks for good things God gives them,
- make treats that celebrate God's goodness, and
- participate in alphabet praises.

YOU'LL NEED

- ❑ small prizes
- ❑ masking tape
- ❑ markers
- ❑ a tray
- ❑ slips of paper
- ❑ balloons
- ❑ office paper that has been used on one side
- ❑ a plate
- ❑ a Bible
- ❑ pencils
- ❑ note cards
- ❑ photocopies of the "Origami Turkey" handout (p. 128)
- ❑ scissors
- ❑ four ingredients of your choice for trail mix
- ❑ spoons

BIBLE BASIS

Psalm 65

This is my favorite of all the psalms. It glows with painterly images and the sense of serene contentment that comes from trusting in a loving, all-powerful God. Because the Hebrew people lived in an agrarian society, they seldom took God's faithfulness for granted. They looked to God for seed, good soil, rain, and sunshine. God's blessing caused flocks and herds to multiply. God's care kept domestic animals from disease and predators. A bountiful harvest was reason to celebrate, for it brought security in the face of the lean winter months to come.

Bible-time folk would be astounded by the abundance we in Western cultures enjoy today. In fact, citizens of most Third World countries would stare in open-mouthed wonder at the variety and volume of food we casually cruise by at local supermarkets. Have you ever known real deprivation over any length of time? I haven't. But I don't want to let the fact that I've always had plenty deprive me of the joy of acknowledging and thanking the Giver.

James 1:17

Do you find pleasure in giving the perfect gift—something that will delight the receiver, reflect the effort you took in creating or finding it, and convey your love and esteem? The gift-giver in you bears the stamp of God's image. God never gives grudgingly or from a sense of obligation. God gives from his abundance of creativity, goodness, and love for us. Let us receive God's good gifts with the same measure of delight with which he gives them.

UNDERSTANDING YOUR KIDS

I wonder how many of your students have missed the experience of eating something that has been picked from a garden just moments before dinner. Today's families constantly run in high gear, with a good percentage of food coming from a drive-in or a cardboard box just removed from the freezer. (My own family is no exception!) Kids almost have to make a leap of faith to realize that they should be giving thanks to God rather than the golden arches! Today's kids may have no idea of how privileged they are to live in this time and this place.

Thanksgiving is a wonderful time to pause and reflect on God's goodness. Use this lesson to help kids realize and rejoice in all the good things that come from God.

The Lesson

Balloon-Pop Prizes

Before class purchase a small, inexpensive prize for each student. For example, you might purchase packs of gum, interesting pens or pencils, small bags of candy such as M&M's, colorful erasers, magnets, giant-sized jawbreakers, or other fun items. (It's OK if several of the prizes are similar.) Use masking tape and a marker to label each prize with a number. Set the prizes on a tray and cover them.

Write matching numbers on slips of paper, put the numbers in separate balloons, then blow up the balloons.

As kids arrive, give them each a marker and a sheet of office paper that's been used on one side. Have kids write their names in large letters on the blank side of their papers then wad the papers into balls. Set a plate in the center of the room and have kids form a large circle around it.

Say: **Do you see those balloons over there? Each balloon contains a number, and each number matches the number of a small prize on that covered tray. You'll each get to choose a balloon, pop it, and get the prize with the matching number.**

Here's how we'll decide who gets to choose a balloon first, second, and so on. The plate in the middle of our circle is a target. When I say, "Toss it," toss your paper wad at the target. I'll open the paper wads that land on and closest to the target, and those people will be the first to pick and pop balloons. We'll choose (the number equaling half the students in your class) **names in the first round. Then those people will sit down with their prizes, and the rest of you will toss again. Are you ready? Toss it!**

Pick up the paper wad closest to the center of the plate, open it, read the owner's name, and let that student pick a balloon. Proceed with the next closest paper wads until half the kids have chosen balloons. Have kids sit or stomp on their balloons to pop them then call out the numbers they find inside. Give students the prizes that match their numbers.

Have the rest of the kids gather their paper wads for the second toss. Call: **Toss it.** Repeat the popping and prize-giving process.

When everyone has a prize, ask:

● **Who do you think had more fun in this game—you or me? Explain.** (We did, because we got prizes; you did, because it was fun for you to watch us play.)

TEACHER TIP

Be sure to have a few extra prizes on hand for visitors. If you're caught short at the last minute, use quarters. Or, if you want to be wildly extravagant, throw in a dollar bill!

Say: **It's fun both to give gifts and to get them. Turn to a partner right now and tell about the best gift you ever received.** Pause for discussion. **Now tell about the best gift you ever gave.** Pause again for discussion. Then ask:

● **Was it easier to remember the best gift you ever received or the best gift you ever gave?** You'll probably receive varying responses.

Say: **Today we're going to learn that ★ all good things come from God. The amazing thing about God is that God just loves to give good things to us. Listen to what the Bible says about that.** Have a volunteer look up and read James 1:17 aloud. **God loves to see us enjoy the things he gives us and he loves to hear us say thank you. Today we're going to have fun saying thank you to God in lots of different ways.**

BIBLE STUDY

A Thanks-Living Psalm (Psalm 65)

Give each student a pencil and another sheet of recycled office paper. Have kids scatter around the room so they're as far as possible from their classmates.

Say: **Listen carefully as I read this psalm of thanksgiving. I'll stop three times and ask you to draw different things, so please fold your paper into three sections. Don't worry if you're not a great artist—no one else will see your drawings. This psalm contains beautiful word pictures. You might want to close your eyes as you listen and try to think of what King David was picturing in his mind as he wrote this beautiful song.**

Read Psalm 65:1-4. Then say: **These verses talk about how God forgives our sins. On one section of your paper, draw a quick sketch to represent something for which God has forgiven you. For example, if God has forgiven you for something you said, you might draw lips or a speech balloon. If you did something that made someone sad, you might draw a sad face. If you put something in first place, ahead of God, you might draw that thing. As you draw, express thanks to God in your heart.**

When most students have finished drawing, give a 30-second warning. Then call time and say: **Please turn your papers over and put them on the floor behind you. Listen as I read the next section of Psalm 65.**

Read Psalm 65:5-8. Then ask:

● **What stood out to you in these verses?** (The beauty of God's creation; God's power; how God takes care of us; the joy

God gives us.)

Say: **These verses mention God's power as shown in creation and the fear and wonder people of all nations experience when they see what God has done. Take a few moments to sketch the part of God's creation that's most awesome to you. It might be a mountain range, a howling storm, a forest, or crashing waves. What have you seen in God's creation that's absolutely awesome?**

Allow a couple of minutes for students to draw. Then call time and say: **Please put your paper and pencil on the floor behind you and listen as I read the final section of this psalm.**

Read Psalm 65:9-13. Then say: **Take a few moments to sketch a beautiful place you've seen that these verses call to mind. Maybe you saw beautiful fields when you took a trip somewhere, or maybe you'll think of a park or a near-by farm or even a flower garden in your own yard. Or maybe you'll think of a Thanksgiving dinner with all your favorite foods. Draw a scene or make a sign with the name of the place you're thinking of.**

When most kids have finished drawing, give a 30-second warning. Then call time and say: **Now form a trio with two people who are sitting near you. Share with your trio one thing you drew on your paper. You don't have to show any pictures; just tell about what you drew and why.**

Walk among students as they share. If younger children are having difficulty getting into the discussion, ask questions such as "What's the most beautiful place you've ever seen?" or "Have you ever visited the seashore? What did you like about it?"

Allow two or three minutes for discussion, then call everyone together and say: **It's easy to pass by some of God's most awesome creations without ever noticing them. God appreciates it when we take time to say thank you and acknowledge that he is the gift-giver. Take your papers and put them with your prizes in the corner. Then join me back here, and we'll make a fun reminder that ★ all good things come from God.**

LIFE APPLICATION

Origami Turkeys

Before class write each of these questions on a separate note card:

● Who's a friend you're especially thankful for?

● What's something in your house that you're especially thankful for?

● What's an ability God has given you that you're especially thankful for?

● What's something about your family that you're especially thankful for?

Practice making the "Origami Turkey" (p. 128) two or three times before class. This project is a bit tricky to fold, but you'll find that the step-by-step drawings take you easily through the process.

Distribute scissors and photocopies of the "Origami Turkey" handout.

Say: **Let's read the verse written in the corner of the large square on your handout.** If there are nonreaders in your class, go over the verse two or three times so they'll learn to "read" it. **Believe it or not, that corner of your handout is about to become the tail of a turkey!**

Have kids cut out the square. Then lead them step by step through the folding process. Have kids who finish early help the others. When everyone has a finished turkey, gather kids in a circle and ask:

● **Why have turkeys become a symbol of giving thanks?** (Because tradition says that Pilgrims and Indians ate turkey at the first Thanksgiving.)

● **Why were the Pilgrims thankful?** (They had traveled safely to the New World; they had crops and food; they had made friends with the helpful Indians.)

Say: **Let's have some fun "stuffing" our turkeys now as we think about things we can be thankful for.**

Place four trail-mix ingredients (such as peanuts, raisins, chocolate chips, butterscotch chips, coconut, banana chips, and M&M's) in four different places in the room. Beside each ingredient, place two spoons and one of the note-card questions.

Say: **Everyone find a partner. I've set up four different stuffing stations containing ingredients for trail mix. At each station you'll find a card with a question on it. The oldest student at each station will read the question aloud. Then, when you and your partner have shared answers to the question, you may both put a spoonful of that ingredient into your turkeys. When I say, "Switch," you and your partner will move clockwise to the next stuffing station.**

Send a similar number of pairs to each station. When all the students have answered the questions and "stuffed" their turkeys, have students move clockwise to the next stuffing station. Continue in this manner until all the pairs have visited all four stations. Then call everyone together.

Say: ★ **All good things come from God, whether they're things we eat, experiences we enjoy, or people we love. If you wish, you may munch on your "stuffing" as we thank God in another fun way.**

126

Alphabet Praises

Say: **Let's celebrate God's goodness with Alphabet Praises. When I say a letter of the alphabet, call out things you're thankful for that start with that letter. You can name anything in God's creation, names of friends and family members, your favorite places to go, or favorite things in your room. Here we go.**

Call out the letters of the alphabet, pausing after each letter for kids to name several things they're thankful for. Settle for one or two things on the more difficult letters. (Xylophone is a great one for the letter X.) When you've completed the alphabet, say: **Well done! It's amazing to think about all the good gifts God has given us. It's important to remember that ★ all good things come from God and to thank God every day for the wonderful things he brings into our lives.**

When you take your turkey home, tell your family how you stuffed it. Do alphabet praises one night at dinner. Stop to notice little things around you that you usually take for granted. Now let's thank God one more way.

CLOSING

One-Word Thanks

Have kids stand in a circle for prayer. Say: **We're going to do a simple closing prayer that you may all have a part in. Think of one word that expresses your thanks to God. For instance, if you wanted to thank God for his love, your one word could be "love." If you wanted to thank God for your family, you'd say "family." Or you could say "provider" if you wanted to thank God for taking care of you. You can pray more than once, but you may say just one word at a time. Let's pray.**

Begin with your own one-word prayer. When most of the children have contributed one or more one-word prayers, close by praying: **We thank you, Lord, for all good things. In Jesus' name, amen.**

Origami Turkey

"Every perfect gift is from God. These good gifts come down from the Creator of the sun, moon, and stars" (James 1:17).

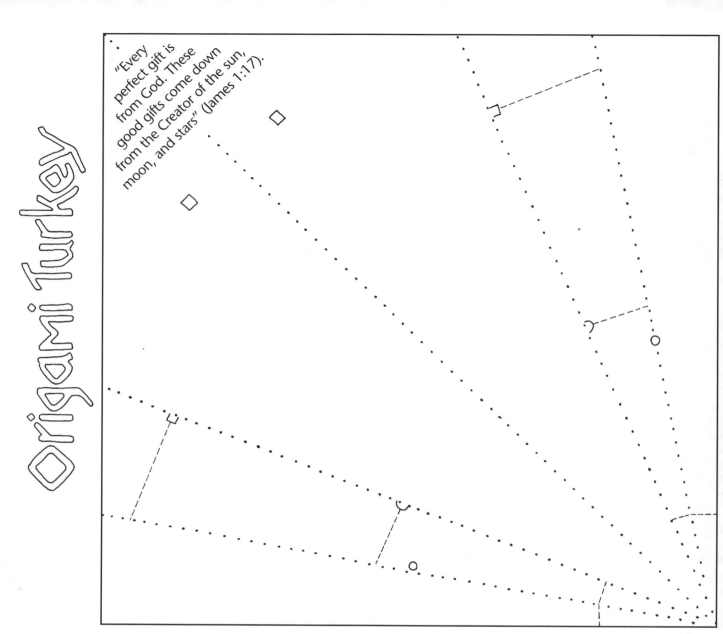

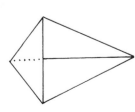

1. Lay the square with the blank side facing you. Fold in half diagonally, then open. Fold two edges to the center.

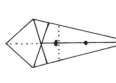

2. Turn the paper over and fold two edges to the center again.

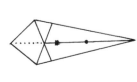

3. Fold the larger end forward at the large square, crease, then unfold.

4. Fold back the smaller end at the large circle.

5. Fold the head forward at the dashed line. Pinch the neck in half, pull the head down, and twist the point of the head to form the turkey's wattle.

6. At the base of the neck, pull the center fold apart so the halves of the large dot touch the small dots. Pinch the base of the neck together and crease well.

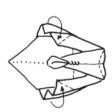

7. At the other end, pull the center apart and pinch the corners so the halves of the large square touch the small squares. Crease on the dashed line.

8. Fold the corners back on the existing creases, then fold the points out again.

Jesus, Our Light

(a lesson for Christmas or for Christmas in July)

LESSON AIM

To help kids understand that ★ Jesus is the light of the world.

OBJECTIVES

Kids or families will
- draw self-portraits in the dark,
- participate in an active Bible story about how Jesus brought light to a world darkened by sin,
- make a craft to remind them that Jesus is the light, and
- plan ways to spread Jesus' light.

YOU'LL NEED

❑ paper
❑ pencils or markers
❑ large paper bags
❑ jingle bells
❑ a Bible
❑ candles
❑ matches
❑ scissors
materials for the learning centers of your choice:
    ❑ a photocopy of the "Pine-Apple Candleholder" handout (p. 136)
      ❑ apples

> ## NOTE
>
> This lesson works well with an intergenerational class. You may wish to invite whole families to join you for this session. Or you might consider using these ideas as the basis for a family Advent night.

- ❑ pine boughs
- ❑ white taper candles
- ❑ paring knives
- ❑ pencils
- ❑ plastic wrap
- ❑ photocopies of the "Candle Paper Sculpture" handout (pp. 137-138)
  - ❑ dark blue, yellow, and white construction paper
  - ❑ rulers·   .
  - ❑ pencils
- ❑ photocopies of the "Jesus Is the Light" handout (p. 139)
  - ❑ transparent tape
  - ❑ pencils
  - ❑ votive candles
- ❑ a photocopy of the "Christmas Sing-Along" handout (p. 140)

BIBLE BASIS

John 1:1-9

This beautiful, highly symbolic Scripture details three core beliefs of the Christian faith: that Jesus was with God from the beginning, that Jesus played a key role in Creation, and that Jesus' mission was to bring light and life to those lost in darkness. Christmas is a season of light. Entire cities deck themselves in decorative lighting. Roofs, bushes, and even barren trees boast tiny, sparkling lights of many hues. The warm glow invites us to welcome once again the tiny child who left the pure light of heaven to enter a world made dark by sin. Jesus' advent, though unnoticed by all but a handful of witnesses, cleaves history in two and marks for all people the starting point of God's great plan of redemption.

Isaiah 9:1-2, 6

Don't you love the words of this passage? Imagine the joy Isaiah experienced when God revealed that he would send a great light into the world that would be for all people, not just the Jews. "No more gloom"—hallelujah!

130

The symbolism of light and darkness is not beyond the grasp of even young children. Kids typically fear dark, shadowy places such as a basement, a closet, or the space under a bed. Kids have also learned to fear the darker side of their own personalities. They know what it's like to throw a tantrum, to get into a fight, and to hurl hurtful words at those they love. With their short span of experience, it's easy for kids to feel that they'll never be any good—that they'll always be the victims of their own sin. Use this lesson to help kids realize that Jesus can replace darkness and fear in their lives with the pure light of his love.

ATTENTION GRABBER

The Lesson

Bag-Heads!

Give each student a sheet of paper, a pencil or marker, and a large paper grocery bag.

Say: **In just a moment, I'm going to give you the opportunity to become something you may never have been before. Congratulations! You're about to become bag-heads!**

Have students slip the bags over their heads.

Say: **Now that you bag-heads are all in the dark, I'm giving you one minute to draw a self-portrait on the paper in front of you. No peeking! Ready? Go!**

After one minute, call time by shaking the jingle bells. Have students write their initials in tiny letters on the back of their portraits. Then collect the paper bags, pencils or markers, and portraits.

Say: **I must say, you're a better-looking group now than you were a moment ago! It's nice to see your smiling faces. Now let's see if we can tell whose faces are represented in these portraits I'm holding.**

Hold up the portraits one by one and let students guess who each portrait represents. Then ask:

● **Why is it so hard to recognize these portraits?** (Because we're not good artists; because we drew them with bags over our heads.)

● **If you'd never met anyone in this class, could you figure out who's who from these portraits? Why or why not?** (No, because the portraits aren't that good; yes, because some people drew special things like glasses or braces.)

TEACHER TIP

Make absolutely sure you use only roomy *paper* bags.

Say: **These portraits aren't too helpful—they leave us in the dark. After all, you drew them in the dark. There was a time long ago when people felt "in the dark" about God too. But God didn't keep his people in the dark. Listen to this promise that God spoke through the prophet Isaiah.**

Read Isaiah 9:2, 6. Then ask:

● **Who is this light that God sent into the world?** (Jesus; God's Son.)

BIBLE STUDY

Darkness to Light (John 1:1-9; Isaiah 9:1-2, 6)

Redistribute the paper grocery bags. Have students scatter around the room so they're as far from each other as possible, then tell them to put on the bags.

Say: **Today we're going to learn that ★ Jesus is the light of the world. Listen carefully for instructions as I tell the story. Freeze as you are and don't move or make any sounds until I tell you to.**

Read the "Darkness to Light" script (p. 133). Read the italicized instructions aloud as part of the story. Follow the directions in parentheses but don't read them aloud.

After you've finished the story, have students blow out their candles and place their paper bags and candles in a corner of the room. Then ask:

● **How was this Christmas story different from other Christmas stories you've heard?** (It started with Creation; it explained why we needed Jesus to come.)

● **Why did we need a Savior to come to earth?** (So we could have our sins forgiven; so we could know what God is like.)

● **How is not knowing Jesus like being in the dark?** (You feel bad because of your sins; you don't have love and joy in your heart.)

● **How does Jesus bring light to our lives?** (He shows us how to live; he takes away our sin; he helps us love each other.)

● **Does anyone have a question about how or why Jesus came to earth?** Discuss as a group any questions that students raise.

● **What customs do we have at Christmastime that remind us that ★ Jesus is the light of the world?** (We put lights on our houses and Christmas trees; we light Advent candles.)

Say: **At Christmastime, we sometimes get so busy that we forget what we're really celebrating. Today we're going to stay focused on the fact that ★ Jesus is the light of the world. And we're going to have fun doing it!**

TEACHER TIP

You may want to play a cassette tape or compact disc of soft, instrumental Christmas music as you read the story. As you light the candles, model quiet, calm behavior. Encourage the children to use both hands to carefully hold the lighted candles in front of them.

Darkness to Light

Long ago, before God created the world, there was nothing but darkness. Then God said, "Let there be light!" *Take off your bags.* And God began creating our beautiful world. God filled the world with wonderful things—beaches and birds, tigers and trees, marshes and mountains, whales and snails, lakes and snakes, dogs and frogs and polliwogs! And last of all, God created people.

God made Adam and put him in a beautiful garden. But God saw that Adam needed a friend, so God created Eve. *Go stand next to another student.*

God and Adam and Eve enjoyed being together in the garden. But one day Eve disobeyed God and ate fruit from a special tree. Suddenly Adam and Eve wanted to hide from God. *Put your bags over your heads and sit down.*

Adam and Eve's sin made God sad. God told them to leave the beautiful garden where they lived. Then another terrible thing happened: One of Adam's sons killed the other son. *Press your fists against your partner's fists.*

Soon sin and darkness were all over the world. Most people didn't love God. (Turn off the lights.) *Wrap your arms around your knees.* People became selfish and wicked and mean. *Turn your back on anyone who's close to you and pound your fists on the floor three times.*

Sometimes God sent special people into the world to teach about his love. People would listen. *Raise your head.* And sometimes they would understand and ask God to forgive them for the wrong things they'd done. *Fold your hands as if you're praying.* And, for a little while, God's light would shine. (Flip the lights on.) *Raise your bag halfway off your head.*

But most people kept on sinning. (Turn the lights off again.) *Pull your bag back over your head.* God was sad because he wanted everyone to live in the light of his love.

Then one day God decided to send into the world a light that would never go out. (Light a candle, then take the bag off one student's head. Give that student a candle and light it.) That light was God's Son, Jesus. (Remove another bag, give that student a candle, and light it. Repeat this process as you continue the story until you've removed all the bags and every student has a glowing candle.)

Jesus came to earth as a tiny baby. He was born in a stable and was placed in a bed of hay. He grew up and ate and slept and studied and worked. Jesus showed us what God is like.

Jesus taught that God loves us and wants us to love each other. *Form a circle.* Jesus said that our sin separates us from God—*blow out your candles*—but that we can ask God to forgive us. Then God will take the sin from our hearts and put his love there instead. (Light the candles of the students on both sides of you.) Jesus taught us to pass God's love on to others. *Pass the flame around the circle.* And Jesus taught that someday we'll live together in heaven where the light from God's face is the only light we'll need. *Hold your candles up.*

LIFE APPLICATION

Celebrate-the-Light Learning Centers

Choose one, two, or all three of these Advent and Christmas learning-center ideas. Each is easy to prepare and fun for kids as well as adults. And each center allows participants to actively explore the important truth that ★ Jesus is the light of the world.

Introduce the learning centers. Allow participants to choose where they'd like to begin. Encourage adults and older kids to work together with younger kids to help them complete their projects. If you have time, let participants do the projects at all three centers; but if you don't have time, offer to send home photocopies of the handouts explaining the projects participants didn't have time to complete.

● **Pine-Apple Candleholder**—Set out the "Pine-Apple Candleholder" handout (p. 136), large red apples, fresh pine boughs, white taper candles, paring knives, pencils, and plastic wrap. Participants will turn apples into beautiful Christmas candleholders by cutting a hole in the top of each apple to hold the base of a candle. Then they'll use pencils to poke holes around the top of the apples and push pine sprigs into those holes. The juice from the apples will keep the pine fresh.

● **Candle Paper Sculpture**—Photocopy the "Candle Paper Sculpture" handout (pp. 137-138). Photocopy the candle pattern onto white paper. Photocopy the flame pattern onto yellow paper. You'll need one candle pattern and one flame pattern for each participant who chooses this craft. Set out scissors, rulers, pencils, and sheets of dark blue construction paper. Participants will cut and assemble the pieces to make a three-dimensional paper sculpture of a glowing candle.

● **Luminarias**—Set out photocopies of the "Jesus Is the Light" handout (p. 139), scissors, tape, pencils, and votive candles. Participants will make luminarias—small bags that glow with the light of a small candle. Tradition says that several luminarias along a road or sidewalk light the way for the wise men.

Announce when there are five minutes of working time left, then two minutes, then one. When you call time with the jingle bells, have participants gather their projects and sit in a circle.

COMMITMENT

Show and Tell

Say: **Form trios with people who are sitting near you. Show the projects you've made and tell how you'll use them.**

Allow trios to share. Then ring the jingle bells to get everyone's attention.

Say: **Today we've learned that ★ Jesus is the light of the world. Listen to these words from the book of Isaiah: "But suddenly there will be no more gloom for the land that suffered...Before those people lived in darkness, but now they have seen a great light. They lived in a dark land, but a light has shined on them...A child has been born to us; God has given a son to us"** (Isaiah 9:1a, 2, 6a).

Turn to the members of your trio and tell one way Jesus' light has shined on you. Pause for trios to share. Then invite participants to tell the whole group what someone else in their trios shared.

Now tell one way you'll spread Jesus' light this week. Allow volunteers to share their plans to spread Jesus' light.

CLOSING

Christmas Sing-Along

Form three groups. Give each group one of the songs from the "Christmas Sing-Along" handout (p. 140). Be sure to give the simpler songs to the groups with the most young children. Have groups practice their songs then take turns teaching them to the whole group.

Close your sing-along with a round of applause for everyone's effort. Then say: **Let's close with a special Christmas greeting. Step up to someone; shake his or her hand; and say, "Jesus is born." The other person will respond, "The light has come." Then say together, "Shine with God's love!"**

Review the greeting once more, then invite participants to give the greeting to at least five people before they leave.

TEACHER TIP

If your students are comfortable with creative movement, you might encourage them to make up hand motions or simple folk dance steps for their songs then perform for or teach the other groups. Or volunteers within a group could be the choreographers and performers.

PINE-APPLE CANDLEHOLDER

Make a living candleholder with a shiny red apple as the base.

● Cut a hole around the stem of the apple about 1 inch deep and large enough to hold the base of a taper candle.

● Use a pencil to poke holes around the top of the apple. Push a sprig of pine into each hole. (The juice from the apple will keep the pine fresh for several days.)

● Carefully push the candle into its hole. If the hole is a bit too large, wrap the base of the candle with plastic wrap.

● Enjoy!

(Caution: Be careful not to let the candle burn low enough to catch the pine on fire.)

CANDLE PAPER SCULPTURE

1. Fold the candle pattern in half on the dotted line. Cut out the candle, including the extension.

2. Fold the flame pattern in half on the dotted line. Cut the flame pattern from A to B, then from C to D. Finally cut slit E.

3. Slip the long strip beneath the flame into the slit near the top of the candle and the extension.

4. Fold a sheet of dark blue construction paper in half lengthwise. Cut half-inch slits at the bottom, three inches from the center fold. Open the paper.

5. Tuck the slits in the candle base into the slits in the blue background paper. Bend the center fold of the candle forward. Bend the center fold of the background back.

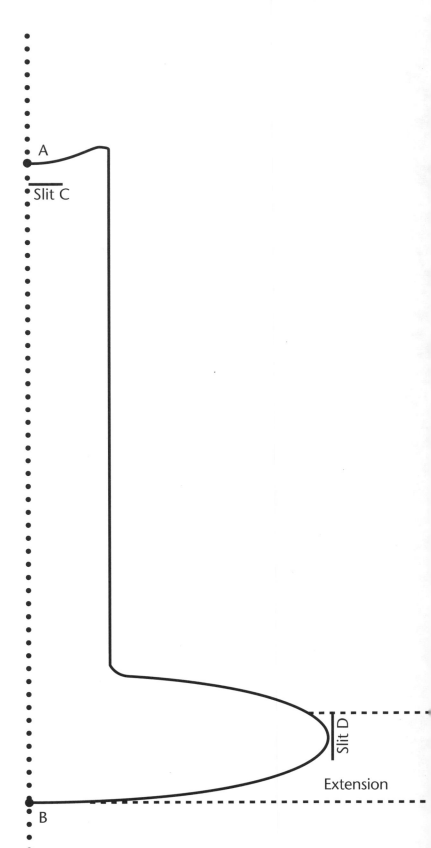

A

Slit C

Slit D

Extension

B

CANDLE PAPER SCULPTURE

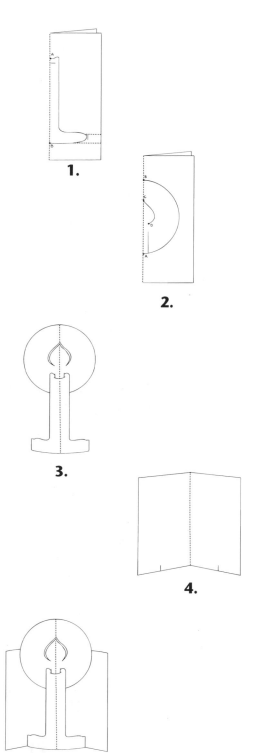

1.

2.

3.

4.

5.

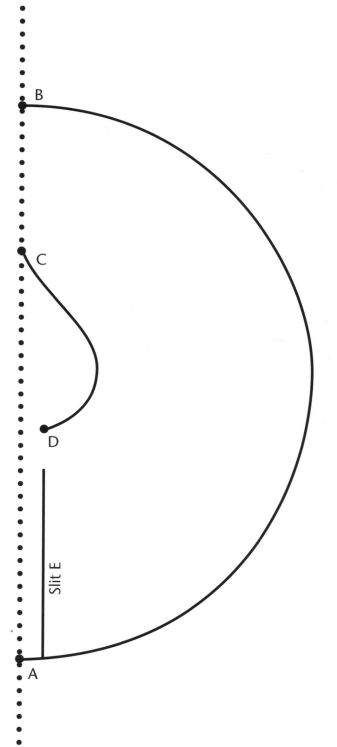

B

C

D

Slit E

A

Tape.

Fold up.

Cut here.

the Light is of the world.

JESUS

Jesus Is the
LIGHT

Photocopy one handout for each person.

A. Use a pencil to poke holes in the star shape.
B. Fold and tape.

C. Fold up the bottom.

D. Push in the corners.

E. Fold the edges over and tape.

F. Pinch and crease the sides at the bottom.
G. Light a candle inside.

JESUS
is
the LIGHT of the World

Fold up.

CHRISTMAS SING-ALONG

(Sing to the tune of "This Little Light of Mine")

Baby Jesus is mine;
I'm gonna let him shine.
Baby Jesus is mine;
I'm gonna let him shine,
Let him shine, let him shine at
Christmastime.

(Sing to the tune of "Jesus Loves Me")

Jesus came from heaven above
To teach us all about God's love.
Jesus came to be our light
And shine within us day and night.
Shine, Lord, in me.
Shine, Lord, in me.
Shine, Lord, in me.
Please shine for all to see.

(Sing to the tune of "Jingle Bells")

(verse)

Jesus came to earth
One night long ago;
Way up high in the sky
A big, bright star did glow.
Precious Son of God
Was born on Christmas night.
And now he lives in heaven above
And helps us spread his light.

(chorus)

Shine through me;
Shine through me;
Dear Jesus, shine through me.
Help me spread your light around
For all the world to see.
Shine through me;
Shine through me;
Dear Jesus, shine through me.
Help me spread your light around
For all the world to see.

Easter Joy!

(a lesson for Easter or any time)

13

LESSON AIM

To help kids understand that ★ Jesus is alive.

OBJECTIVES

Kids will
- discover how Jesus' disciples felt when Jesus died and rose again,
- hear the Easter story from Mary Magdalene's perspective,
- make personal reminders of Jesus' resurrection, and
- enjoy an Easter celebration.

YOU'LL NEED

- ❑ a paper bag of various household items
- ❑ a dishpan of water
- ❑ a towel
- ❑ a photocopy of the "Mary, Jesus' Friend" story (pp. 145-146)
- ❑ scissors
- ❑ Bibles

materials for the learning centers of your choice:
- ❑ photocopies of the "Pop-Up Critter" handout (p. 151)
  - ❑ 3×5 cards
  - ❑ markers
- ❑ photocopies of the "Easter Lily Pop-Up" handout (p. 152)
  - ❑ scissors
  - ❑ half-sheets of green construction paper
  - ❑ glue sticks
- ❑ paper plates for "Name-in-a-Rainbow"
  - ❑ a bowl of water
  - ❑ white crayons
  - ❑ a spray bottle of water

❏ paintbrushes
❏ cups of thinned red, yellow, and blue tempera paint
❏ newsprint
❏ a marker

BIBLE BASIS

John 20:1-18

Jesus' closest friends had spent nearly three years in his company. They thought it nothing to give up homes, careers, and financial resources for the privilege of being close to the Messiah, God's chosen Savior. When Jesus was arrested, mocked, interrogated, and beaten by the Temple guards, the exciting life of these followers crumbled around them. And as an earthquake signaled Jesus' death on the cross, their world spun tragically out of control. How could it be? Why did he allow it? What should they do next? Run. Hide. Lock the doors.

But they couldn't hide forever. So on Sunday morning, Mary Magdalene made her way to the tomb to anoint Jesus' body—the one last service she could perform for her Lord. The unthinkable had happened. Jesus' body was gone! Mary ran to inform the disciples, then returned to the tomb to weep. When a kind man approached her, Mary, thinking he was a gardener, pleaded with him to tell her where Jesus' body had been taken. "Mary," the man replied. Mary instantly recognized Jesus, her risen Lord. The tragedy and gloom of Friday dissolved in the glory of Easter morning!

Easter gives us hope. Jesus' death and resurrection form the very core of our Christian beliefs. Jesus made the way for us—we only have to follow. Because of Easter, we can erase "impossible" and "hopeless" from our vocabulary. The power that raised Jesus from the dead is at work in us. *Anything* is possible. Hallelujah!

Luke 8:1-3

Mary Magdalene was one of a small group of women who followed Jesus out of love and gratitude for the help and healing he'd provided. These women also supported Jesus and the Twelve Apostles with their financial resources. It couldn't have been an easy life following Jesus from city to city. Their faithful, grateful lifestyle sets an example for all Christians.

Do you remember feeling powerless as a child? Feeling that grown-ups would make all the decisions, right or wrong, and that you just had to resign yourself to whatever might happen? Worrying that a psychopath would enter your home and harm you? Fearing a tragic accident? Wondering if a fatal disease would invade the body of someone you loved?

All kids know these feelings. The antidote? An eye-opening, life-changing glimpse of the love and power of our *living* God. God spoke, light shattered the dark void of space, and the universe came to be. That same God put his very essence into the body of a tiny human child. When the child grew to manhood, evil did its best to defeat him. But Jesus broke the chains of death and, with his victory, brought us eternal life. Kids need to know that this living God can be their daily companion and that, because Jesus lives, they have nothing to fear in this life *or* the next.

The Lesson

ATTENTION GRABBER

Can't Keep Me Down

Before class gather several small, household items in a paper bag. Kids will guess whether each item will sink or float in a dishpan of water. You might include an eraser, a pencil, a peanut in a shell, a grape, a paper clip, a quarter, a pair of scissors, a stone, a cork, a toothpick, a nail, a rubber band, or whatever else you can quickly rummage from your "junk drawer"!

As kids arrive greet them by saying: **Christ is risen.** Teach them to respond, "He is risen indeed," then exchange high fives. Encourage kids to repeat this greeting with each other as students arrive.

After everyone has arrived and been greeted, say: **We're here to celebrate the greatest event in history. Death is doomed, and ★ Jesus is alive! Jesus' enemies killed him on a cross, but Jesus had the last word! Nothing could keep him down. Let's do a couple of fun things to remind us of Jesus' resurrection.**

Have kids stand facing a wall with their toes about six inches from the base of the wall. Demonstrate how to hold your arms rigid and press the backs of your wrists hard against the wall. Once everyone is in position, count: **One thousand one, one** thousand two, and so on up to 30. Then have kids step back from the wall and relax their arms. Because of the built-up muscle tension, everyone's arms will want to "float" upward. This is a truly strange experience even for those who have done it before! Gather kids in a circle and ask:

● **What was it like when your arms floated upward?** (Weird; cool; I could hardly believe it.)

● **How does this activity remind you of Jesus' resurrection?** (Our arms rose up; we couldn't keep our arms down.)

Say: **Let's have some more fun with things that rise.**

Set out a dishpan of water. Set the bag of household items next to it. Let kids take turns drawing an item from the bag without looking. After a child chooses an item, let him or her predict whether it will sink or float then test it by dropping it in the water. Have a towel nearby to dry the items and children's hands.

Ask:

● **Does anyone whose item floated think you can make it sink by adding anything to the dishpan?**

Let volunteers try to make their items sink. (Unless they're smarter than I am, they won't succeed!) Ask:

● **Why are some things just determined to float?** (Because of what they're made of; because that's the way God made them.)

● **How does this activity remind you of Jesus' resurrection?** (The floating things couldn't be kept down just as death couldn't keep Jesus down; Jesus rose from the dead the way the floating things rose in the water.)

Say: **Nothing could keep Jesus down—not even death. That's why we're celebrating today. But when Jesus died, his followers didn't understand that he would rise from the dead three days later. Let's look at the Easter story from their perspective and see if we can understand what they thought and felt during the events of Good Friday and Easter Sunday.**

BIBLE STUDY

Mary, Jesus' Friend (Luke 8:1-3; John 20:1-18)

Before class photocopy the "Mary, Jesus' Friend" story (pp. 145-146). Cut apart the 12 verses.

Have students form pairs. If there are nonreaders in your class, be sure to pair them with readers. Distribute the verses of the story as evenly as possible among the pairs.

Say: **Decide which partner will be the reader and which partner will lead the motions. I'll give you a couple of minutes to go over your verses together.**

Mary, Jesus' Friend

(based on Luke 8:1-3 and John 20:1-18)

1

Do you know what happened
  when Jesus died?
(Put arms out like a cross.)
Just a few friends stayed at his side.
Afraid of the soldiers, most ran
  away.
(Pretend to run.)
But Jesus' friend Mary chose to
  stay.

2

Once Mary's life had been full of
  sin,
But Jesus had made her all clean
  within.
(Press hands over heart.)
He took all the sins in her heart
  away,
And they'd been good friends since
  that happy day.
(Hug your partner.)

3

When Jesus went preaching from
  town to town,
The 12 disciples followed him
  around.
(Make your fingers "walk.")
Mary and her friends would come
  along too,
To see the great things that Jesus
  would do.
(Point and look surprised.)

4

He healed the sick and made the
  lame walk,
And everyone wanted to hear Jesus
  talk!
(Cup hands around ears.)
He spoke of his Father in heaven
  above
(Point up.)
And told about God's great kind-
  ness and love.

5

Everywhere Jesus and his followers
  went,
People would pray to God and
  repent.
(Fold hands as if praying.)
"Jesus is Lord," they'd all agree.
(Nod your head.)
"He takes away sins and makes the
  blind see."

6

But one day some bad men took
  Jesus away.
(Pretend to drag someone away.)
They put him on trial that very sad
  day.
(Shake your head and look sad.)
"Will they hurt my Lord?" Mary
  wondered aloud.
"Just look at the angry folks in this
  crowd!"

(continued)

145

7

"They can't take Jesus! Oh, what a loss!"
Mary cried softly at the foot of his cross.
(Rub your eyes as if crying.)
"What shall we do? Where shall we go?
Look—now he has died! Oh, no! Oh, no!"
(Cover your face and shake your head.)

8

On Sunday Mary went to the tomb.
When she got there, she saw just an empty room.
(Pretend to peek in the tomb.)
"They've taken his body!" Mary said.
But an angel said, "Jesus rose from the dead!"
(Look surprised.)

9

Mary stayed near the tomb, quite close by.
Then a man said, "Woman, why do you cry?"
"They've taken my Lord," she said with a tear.
"Do you know where he is? I can't find him here."
(Shrug shoulders as if asking a question.)

10

"Mary," he said in a voice soft and kind.
"It's Jesus!" she thought, joy filling her mind.
(Put hands to cheeks in surprise.)
"Rabboni! My teacher! Can it be you?
The news that the angel spoke really is true!"

11

Jesus said, "Now you must go tell my brothers."
So off Mary ran to tell all the others.
(Pretend to run.)
"I have seen Jesus. He spoke my name!
Now nothing will ever again be the same."

12

Mary loved Jesus right to the end.
(Press hands over heart.)
Even at the cross, she was his friend.
Did you know that you can be Jesus' friend, too?
Just as Jesus loved Mary, he also loves you!
(Hug yourself.)

Have all the pairs stand in one circle in the order their verses fall in the story. Explain that everyone should do the motions with the pair that's performing.

When pairs are ready, introduce the story by saying: **Now we're ready to go back in time to the saddest day in all history—the day Jesus died.**

Signal the pair with the first verse to begin.

At the end of the story, lead everyone in a round of applause. Then have the class scatter around the room in their pairs. Ask these questions, pausing after each one to allow partners time for discussion.

● **Why did so few of Jesus' friends stand by him when he was on the cross?** (They were afraid; they didn't want to be arrested.)

Say: **The Bible tells us that four women, including Jesus' mother and Mary Magdalene from our story, stayed by the cross. So did the Apostle John.** Ask:

● **Why did these people stay by Jesus when nearly everyone else ran away and hid?** (Because they loved him so much; they wanted to comfort Jesus; they were brave.)

● **If you had been alive then, do you think you would've stayed by Jesus or stayed out of sight? Explain.** (I'd have been scared and hidden somewhere; I might have stayed; I'm not sure.)

● **Why did Jesus' followers love him so much?** (Because he told them about God's love; because Jesus loved them first; because he healed them and took away their sins.)

Call everyone together and let volunteers report on their discussions. Then say: **Listen to Luke 8:1-3. It tells us how Mary Magdalene came to be Jesus' friend.** Read the passage from an easy-to-understand version of the Bible. Then ask:

● **What does this passage tell us about Mary Magdalene?** (That Jesus cast seven demons out of her.)

Say: **Before Mary met Jesus, her life was filled with evil and pain. But Jesus changed all that. Mary was heartbroken when Jesus died. But she also had the honor of being the first person Jesus spoke to after he rose from the dead. We can know the same joy Mary knew, because ★ Jesus is alive today!**

LIFE APPLICATION

Easter-Joy Learning Centers

Say: **Jesus can change our lives just as he changed Mary's.** Ask:

● **Who can tell me how Jesus can change our lives today?** (He forgives our sins and makes us clean inside; he can make us part of God's family; he gives us eternal life in heaven.)

Say: **Jesus can take away our sins and fill our hearts with God's love. And when Jesus rose from the dead, he conquered death for all of us who believe in him. That means we can look forward to living in heaven forever. And that's reason to celebrate!**

Before class review the three learning-center ideas explained below. You may want to set up one, two, or all three centers. Each is fun and easy to prepare and will help students understand and celebrate Jesus' resurrection.

Introduce the learning centers and show kids what they can make at each one. Then allow students to choose where they'll begin. If you have time, students may enjoy doing all three activities.

● **Pop-Up Critter**—Children will be charmed by these irrepressible little pop-up creatures. The harder you push them down, the higher they pop up! Set out 3×5 cards, photocopies of the "Pop-Up Critter" handout (p. 151), markers, and a sample of the finished critter.

Explain that Jesus' enemies tried to keep him down, but even after they killed him, he rose from the dead. Just like the little pop-up critter, Jesus couldn't be held down!

● **Easter Lily Pop-Up**—Students make a beautiful card with a pop-up lily inside. Photocopy the "Easter Lily Pop-Up" handout (p. 152) on plain white paper. Set out the photocopies, scissors, half-sheets of dark green construction paper for the background, glue sticks, and a sample of the completed card.

Explain that lilies appear to die after a hard frost, but the next year they pop up again and bloom, serving as a vibrant reminder of Jesus' victory over death.

● **Name-in-a-Rainbow**—Students make beautiful rainbows on paper plates with Jesus' name showing through the rainbow. Set out paper plates; a bowl of water; a spray bottle of water; white crayons; paintbrushes; and cups of thinned red, yellow, and blue tempera paint.

Have kids write "Jesus" in white crayon on paper plates. It's important to press hard and go over the name three or four times. Then have students mist the plates with a light spray of water. The plates should be damp but without puddles. Demonstrate how to swish a generous brush stroke of each color of tempera paint on the damp plate. Then tip the plates so the primary colors run together, forming all the colors of the rainbow. The wax from the crayon will resist the paint, so Jesus' name will shine through the rainbow!

Explain that Jesus' friends wrapped his body in a cloth but that Jesus didn't stay hidden. Just as the letters show through the colors, Jesus rose from the dead and showed himself to hundreds of people!

Circulate among students as they work. Ask:

- **What makes Easter special to you?**
- **Why is it important that Jesus rose from the dead?**
- **How does this remind you of Jesus' resurrection?**

As your learning-center time draws to a close, give a five-minute warning, then three minutes, then one. If children seem disappointed by not having time to do all the crafts, you may want to offer them handouts for the crafts they didn't have time to complete.

COMMITMENT

Live It!

Gather everyone in a circle. Have kids set their crafts behind them, outside the circle, so they won't be a distraction. Ask:

- **What have you learned today?** (That Jesus is alive; that Jesus' enemies couldn't keep him down.)

Say: ★ **Jesus is alive! And he can make a difference in our lives every day. Even though we can't see him, Jesus can be our closest friend.** Ask:

- **Think about your three closest friends—what are some things you do with them?** (Play; talk on the phone; eat together; stay overnight at their houses.)

- **Since ★ Jesus is alive and Jesus is our friend, too, what are some things we can do with him each day?** (Talk to him in prayer; remember that he's always with us; ask for his help.)

Say: **It's a wonderful thing to have a friend like Jesus. Let's discover some of the things Jesus promises his followers. Listen for the little phrase that's repeated in each of these Scriptures.**

Write these references on a large sheet of newsprint: John 14:16; John 14:27; and Matthew 28:18-20. Have volunteers look up the passages and read them aloud. The repeated phrase is "with you." Ask:

- **What does it mean to you that Jesus is with you every day?** (It makes me feel good; it makes me want to live so he'll be proud of me; I can be strong and brave.)

Say: **Turn to a partner and tell him or her one thing you'll do differently this week because you know that ★ Jesus is alive and he's with you wherever you go.**

Give kids a few moments to share. Then ask volunteers to share their partners' comments.

CLOSING

Easter Rap

Say: **Let's close our class with a special Easter rap. I'll say a line, then you repeat it after me and do what I do.**

Jesus is alive! *(Point upward, then pull down strong fists.)*
Gimme a high five. *(Give someone a high five.)*
They tried to keep him down *(push down with both hands)*
In a cave in the ground. *(Make an arch like a cave entrance with hands.)*
But could they do it? No way? *(Shake finger.)*
He's alive today! *(Point up and shake arms three times.)*

Do the rap several times so kids learn the words and the rhythm. Then form two groups and have them stand in lines facing each other. Let one group lead the rap as the other group echoes each line. Then let the other group lead.

Call everyone together in a tight circle and make a pile of hands. Close with a prayer similar to this one: **Dear Lord Jesus, thank you for giving your life for our sins. Thank you for conquering death for us. Help us live every day for you and remember that you're alive and that you're our friend. Amen.**

Pop-up Critter

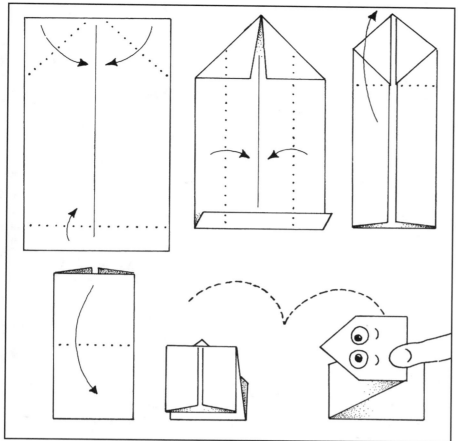

1. Fold a 3×5 card in half length-wise, then unfold it.
2. Fold the two top corners to the middle as if you were making a paper airplane.
3. Fold the bottom up about ½ inch.
4. Fold both sides into the middle.
5. Fold the bottom over the top at the base of the diamond.
6. Fold the bottom edge back to the middle.
7. Turn your critter over and draw a face on it.
8. Have a poppin' good time and remember: Even death couldn't keep Jesus down!

Pop-up Critter

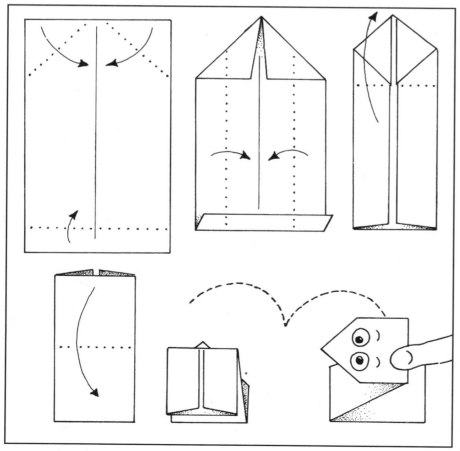

1. Fold a 3×5 card in half length-wise, then unfold it.
2. Fold the two top corners to the middle as if you were making a paper airplane.
3. Fold the bottom up about ½ inch.
4. Fold both sides into the middle.
5. Fold the bottom over the top at the base of the diamond.
6. Fold the bottom edge back to the middle.
7. Turn your critter over and draw a face on it.
8. Have a poppin' good time and remember: Even death couldn't keep Jesus down!

Permission to photocopy this handout granted for local church use. Copyright © Lois Keffer. Published in *Sunday School Specials 3* by Group Publishing, Inc., Box 481, Loveland, CO 80539.

EASTER LILY PoP-uP

Photocopy this handout on white paper. Fold it in half on the dotted line and cut around the solid line from A to B. Fold a half-sheet of green construction paper, then open it. Center the fold of the lily over the fold of the green construction paper. Fold back the tabs at the bottom of the lily, rub them with a glue stick, and press them in place on the background paper. Pull the fold of the lily forward. When you fold the card, the lily will disappear inside. When you open the card, the lily will pop up.

B

Fold tabs back and glue to background.

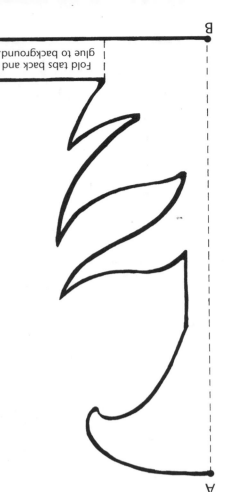

A

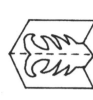

EASTER LILY PoP-uP

Photocopy this handout on white paper. Fold it in half on the dotted line and cut around the solid line from A to B. Fold a half-sheet of green construction paper, then open it. Center the fold of the lily over the fold of the green construction paper. Fold back the tabs at the bottom of the lily, rub them with a glue stick, and press them in place on the background paper. Pull the fold of the lily forward. When you fold the card, the lily will disappear inside. When you open the card, the lily will pop up.

B

Fold tabs back and glue to background.

A

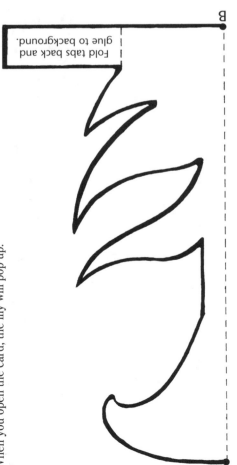